Coda

to

The Setup and Repair of the Double Bass
For Optimum Sound

by

Chuck Traeger

New Sound Setup Discoveries
&
Repair Tips

First Edition 2009

Henry Strobel, Violin Maker & Publisher
Aumsville, Oregon 97325

www.HenryStrobel.com

First Edition, August 2009

Library of Congress Control Number: 2009932009

ISBN-13:   978-1-892210-10-4

Printed in the United States of America
Reprinted June 2010

Charles (Chuck) Traeger
PO Box 187
Yulan, New York 12792
USA

Cover photos and design by Kelly L. Merchant and William Merchant

TABLE OF CONTENTS

Dedication iv
Sixword by Ron Carter v
Prologue vi

I - SETUP
Chapters 1 Thru 9

1   Before You Start 10
2   The Endpin – Mightier than the Sound Post 12
3   The Heart and Soul of the Bass or How to
      Make the Bass Louder and More Responsive 16
4   Simplifying Mode Matching 21
5   Making a Bass Brighter or Darker 24
6   More About Sound Posts 26
7   Strings 29
8   Putting On the Strings 31
9   Things that Hurt the Sound 32

II - REPAIR
Chapters 10 thru 19

10   Before Beginning a Major Repair or Overhaul 35
11   A Shrunken Back Repair 36
12   Five String Neck Thicknesses 37
13   Stand Height 38
14   Flat Back Crossbars 39
15   Alternate Methods 40
16   Don't Be Upset When 43
17   Self Service Repairs 46
18   White Glue Warning 48
19   Mission Impossible 51

III - ANCILLARIA
Chapters 20 thru 24

20   Protocols 53
21   Travel Tip 54
22   Repairer's Oath 55
23   The Must Be 3 C's 56
24   The Quest 57

Epilogue 59
Thank You 63

Dedication

I want to dedicate this short book to the three modern repairmen without whose help this book would never have been properly finished. They are David Brownell for his excellent editorial comments, Bill Merchant for the pictures and his help with my research, and help in organizing the book, Gary Rickman for his many helpful suggestions and his experimental work, and bassist Ron Carter, the ultimate listener, for his friendship and support, and his constant search for more, which helped lead me to my sound discoveries.

It is my sincere hope that these three repairmen's successes will inspire other repairers to follow in their footsteps for the betterment of the instrument I love, and it is my further hope that bass players will listen as critically as Ron Carter and ask for more. I dedicate this booklet to all of you.

And a final dedication to the memory of Carleen Hutchins,
my friend.

Bass Photos

Eighteenth Century Italian Bass .... *front cover*
English, Samuel Allen, owned and played by Gary Peacock viii
Giuseppe Lecchi, Genoa, Italy, 1929 11
John Frederick Lott, London 15
Barbe, pere, France 28
James Cole, Manchester, England 30
Ron Carter's main bass, Anton Schroetter, Mittenwald 32
Eighteenth Century Italian Bass 38, 42
Gagliano (attributed), Royal Concertgebouw, ex Homer Mensch 44
George Lotte (worked under J. B. Vuillaume), France, 19th C. ... 45
Fausto Casalini, Faenza, Italy, December, 1925 50
Anthony Posch, Vienna, 1729 54
John Betts, England, 1833 62
Fausto Casalini, Lion's head on bass pictured on page 49 63

(Courtesy of Bill Merchant's photo collection of basses he has worked on)

iv

Sixword
by
Ron Carter

When I finished writing my first book, I asked Ron Carter if he would write a foreword for it. He said, "No." I was shocked and disappointed until he immediately added, "But I'll write a fiveword." And he did. When I finished this booklet I asked him again to write something. Six comes after five, so here is his Sixword -

Having lived in New York City for over 40 years, and having all sorts of work done, my instrument has always been a concern of mine. How will the answers to the following questions affect the sound of my bass:

1...What is that rattle?
2...Does the sound post need to be adjusted *again*?
3...Is the saddle too low?
4...Can the groove in the fingerboard be eliminated?
5...Can this crack be repaired without talking the top off?
6...What do the latest strings sound like?
7...Is my bridge warped?
8...What other kind of endpin can I try?
9...How will Teflon pads under my bridge feet affect my sound?

As I said, having lived in New York City for over 40 years, and having all sorts of work done invariably my instrument has always been a concern of mine. So, I call Chuck Traeger for the answers to questions 1 thru 9 because he has always had all the answers to my questions about sound.

Ron Carter

Prologue

About the title, the dictionary definition of the word 'coda' is:

> *music;* A: a concluding passage, the function of which is to bring a composition to a cogent and well-proportioned close.

My wife, June, suggested this title because that is exactly what I am doing here. This booklet is the conclusion of my research and my writing. It is not that there is no more to be done. It is that at eighty three I am running out of the time to do it.

Before I go any further I want to make something very clear. This is not a scientific booklet, nor even a semi scientific booklet. The reason for this is simple. I am not writing for scientists. I am writing for bass players and repairers who, for the most part, couldn't tell a phase from a vase, and who couldn't care less. I am reminded of what happened years ago in my shop. I was explaining what I was going to do and why to a member of the New York Philharmonic when he suddenly interrupted me and said, "Don't tell me about it, just do it." So while this is a 'tell me about it' booklet, it is more a 'do it' booklet. In other words it is a PRACTICAL booklet based on empirical observation rather than scientifically corroborated facts. And if you 'do it' you will be pleasantly surprised and remain a happy bass player.

Thoreau in his book, *On Walden Pond* wrote three words I have never forgotten. "Simplify, Simplify, Simplify." That is what I have tried to do in this booklet.

Something has been bothering me for quite a while. Every time I pick up a copy of a magazine devoted to the bass I see on the cover a picture of one of the bass world's bright stars with their instrument. But as I look at the picture of the bass I see that there is something wrong with the setup, something which could be easily corrected to make the bass sound better. The player obviously hasn't read my big book, *The Setup and Repair of the Double Bass for Optimum Sound.* So I decided to write this little booklet with all the setup information in one easy to read place in the hope that these players will read it and benefit by it.

First, it contains new information that I have discovered since the publication of my book, and, second, it was further prompted by an experience of a general repairer who had just begun to work on basses using my methods. He did a wonderful restoration on a bass making the sound 'big enough to fill a house.' But the sound wasn't the one the owner wanted to hear. It was too dark, too rich. He wanted a brighter sound. Unfortunately, the repairer hadn't read the part of my book on setup, and so didn't know what to do until he called me and explained his problem. I told him what to do, and all turned out well in the end. So for the repairer as well as the player I decided to put all the setup information in one easy to find place - the first part of the book.

The new material and the rest of the setup information are based on what I have come to call **Traeger's Principle** which states:

When a bass is being played EVERYTHING is vibrating, from the top of the scroll to the tip of the endpin.

First corollary: For Optimum Sound to occur every part of the bass must be vibrating at an optimum level and in sync (in phase) with its neighbors so that it reinforces the vibrations of its neighbors rather than conflicting with them.

Second corollary: Maximum is **not** necessarily Optimum.

For example, when the neck is too thin it will vibrate at maximum level siphoning off energy from the strings, which should have gone into the top to increase resonance. My friend, colleague, and coauthor David Brownell reminds me that there is another element in play. A neck that is too thin, which vibrates at maximum amplitude level, may have pushed the characteristic vibration frequency of the neck out of the register where it can usefully reinforce the overall sound of the instrument (Mode Matching) to increase volume. See Chapter 10, Mode Matching, in my book, or read Chapter 5, Simplifying Mode Matching, here for an explanation of this effect. This latter effect may have, I believe, a less negative impact than the energy displacement mentioned above.

Most of the rest of this booklet is dedicated to helpful hints on repairing. However, I wrote the last two chapters in an effort to describe and explain my love for this instrument. Therefore, I consider this booklet a necessary postscript to my first book. In so far as anything can be final, this finishes my research on Optimum Sound.

I wish to add this. I have been heartened by news trickling in that repairers, especially the next generation, are beginning to repair using my methods. I have also been troubled by something. I know of two of these successful repairers who report they can't hear what I have been able to hear because they were never professional bass players. In fact, one of them told me that he had to rely on the aural observations of his customers when he was setting up a bass.

So this is my advice to would be repairers. If you want to be a true master repairer you should be able to hear what your repairs and adjustments are doing. Take bass lessons and practice at least one hour a day for at least a year. Also try to get into a jazz band and play with them. As Francois Rabbath once remarked, "Play jazz, even if it's bad jazz. It teaches you to listen." If you listen critically you will hear.

If you bought my first book you will remember that the bass pictured on the cover has been split in two. The left side shows the top on, ready to be setup properly. The right has the top off, ready to be repaired properly. The bass pictured on the cover of this book has been repaired, setup, and is ready to make music. It is finished and, as such, it represents the finish of my personal search for Optimum Sound. That doesn't mean there isn't more. There is always more, always more.

One final note (bass clef naturally) - I enjoy helping people so feel free to call me. My phone is 845 557 6352 from 11 AM to 11 PM Eastern time. Call! Enjoy this booklet. Enjoy your bass.

P.S. About the word 'Ancillaria', which heads the third section of this book - I said in my first book, *The Setup and Repair of the Double Bass for Optimum Sound*, that if you can't have fun doing what you are doing you shouldn't be doing it. Well, I enjoy writing because I know that I will be disseminating knowledge that will be useful for repairers and players alike for decades and perhaps even longer. And I have tried to write with a sense of occasional humor.

I am blessed to be able to write in the English language because it is in a state of flux, perhaps more so than any other language. Meanings change. Pronunciations change. Words are constantly dying and being born every day. So I had fun aiding this latter process with the invention and introduction of the word 'ancillaria.' Perhaps it may even catch on.   *ancillaria: material subordinate to and/or in addition to what has gone before*

What may be the only bass made by famed English bow maker, Samuel Allen, as stamped and labeled (owned and played by Gary Peacock, on which I have worked).

I - SETUP

CHAPTERS 1 thru 9

Chapter 1

Before You Start

There are several things that should be checked to see if they have been done to the bass properly before anything else is considered. The reason for this is that these basic adjustments will set the bass up for the final adjustments producing Optimum Sound.

First, check the spacing of the strings at the nut. It should be no more than 3/8ths of an inch (9 mm.) from the center of the strings. If the spacing is any more than that, now is the time to correct it. The reason behind this is simple - the strings of the bass act somewhat like the guy wires on a cell phone tower. The wider the stays are placed at the foot of the tower the more force they will exert against lateral movement and thus the more rigid the tower will be, and vice-versa. The wider the strings at the nut the more the outside G and E strings will stiffen the neck and make it more rigid and less able to vibrate properly. See Chapter 8 in my first book, *The Setup and Repair of the Double Bass for Optimum Sound.*

Also check to see if the strings' spacing at the bridge is no more than 1 1/16th of an inch (27 mm.) - 1 inch (25 mm.) is even better - measured center to center, although the narrower spacing may raise the A and D strings too high off the fingerboard. The reason for this is the same as for the nut spacing. The smaller the spacing the more easily it is for the bridge to vibrate properly. If the bridge is so low that such a spacing would make the bow hit the side of the bass, the spacing can be made wider. The spacing is measured center to center because the fingers for pizzicato and the bow hairs for arco hit the top center of the strings. This makes for a more uniform feel for the right hand.

Also check the thickness of the bridge top. Less than six millimeters increases the chances of future warping.

Second, check the thickness of the neck-fingerboard. It should be 1 ½ inches (38 mm.) at the A note on the G string and 1 3/4ths of an inch (44 mm.) at the D note on the G string, or as close as you can come to that note before the neck starts its curve into the neck butt. Too thick or too thin a neck will interfere with Optimum Sound by not vibrating at optimum level. Too thick will vibrate at only minimum level; too thin at maximum level. Optimum is somewhere in between, and it varies with each bass.

Third, check to see that the width of the bridge feet is such that the center of the E foot of the bridge is directly over the center of the bass bar, or as close to it as possible. This is because the E foot acts like a piston on the bass bar and acts most efficiently when the center of the E foot is directly over the center of the bass bar. This is important because different basses have different sizes and thus different bass bar locations. One sized bridges will not fit all bass bar locations. Also, check to see that the bridge is centered over the center of the top of the bass and not off to one side or the other. This could affect the sound adversely by making the G string louder than the E string, or vice-versa.

Check to see that the strings at the nut rest just barely above the fingerboard. The higher they are the harder it is for the left hand to press them down. Also check the fingerboard itself to make sure that the end to end camber is not too deep making the strings at the middle of the board hard to depress, or too shallow possibly causing the strings to buzz And check the entire board lengthwise to make sure there are no hills or valleys in it which might make one or more notes buzz. The fingerboard for its entire length should be one long even curve.

Finally, for a three quarter size instrument the neck angle above the top of the bass should be such that the optimum bridge height is 6 ¾ inches (171 mm.). Too high a bridge will produce a nasal sound on the G string and an overbearingly loud sound on the E string. However, this can be compensated for by making a high saddle. See Chapter 12 in my first book. Furthermore, the neck should be over the center of the top, not off to one side or the other. If it is too far off it can be compensated for by 'faking the bridge'. While I did not call this procedure 'faking the bridge' in my book I did describe what has to be done. With the bridge feet centered on the top, one leg or the other of the bridge is shortened to make the top of the bridge lean until it is centered with respect to the center of the fingerboard. See Chapter 17 in my first book. Too low a bridge will produce a mushy, uncentered sound. But since this problem may mean a major repair involving a neck reset to make for proper neck angle, it is not absolutely necessary to do. Everything else is.

A bass made by Giuseppe Lecchi in Genoa , Italy in 1929, as labeled.

Chapter 2

The Endpin – Mightier than the Sound Post

A bass endpin has a strong effect, not only on the overall volume of the instrument but also on the tone quality. By experimenting with endpin rod materials you can significantly increase the volume of your bass and change the tone color to suit your individual needs. In fact, sometimes it is possible to produce two different tone colors by having and changing two different types of wood endpin rods. And this is something you can do yourself!

I was very gratified to read a while back an article in the International Society of Bassists magazine, Bass World, detailing an experiment by Laborie and Rabbath inserting an endpin in a bass at an angle rather than straight out. It was during this experiment that they discovered that metal is a very poor material for an endpin. This is something I have been preaching for over thirty years. The only thing that is worse than a straight metal endpin is a bent one.

The adjustable metal endpin first began to appear about the beginning of the 20th century. At that time the manufacturers, repairmen and makers who began to use it considered it only as a piece of furniture to adjust the height of the bass to the players' comfort. It never once occurred to any of them that the endpin played a vital function in the sound of the bass.

What I have come to call **Traeger's Principle** states: "When a bass is being played, EVERYTHING is vibrating, from the top of the scroll to the tip of the endpin. For Optimum Sound to occur every part of the bass must be vibrating at an optimum level and in sync (in phase) with its neighbors so that it reinforces the vibrations of its neighbors rather than conflicting with them." Metal does not even come close to optimum vibration because it is too stiff to vibrate properly. A metal endpin is like a water pipe. Put a bend in the water pipe and less water will flow through because of the increased resistance imposed by the bend. Put a bend in a metal endpin and fewer vibrations will pass through for the same reason.

The heavier the metal rod the less it will vibrate and the further it will depart from optimum vibration. The same can be said for large hollow metal rod endpins.

Why did I state that the endpin is mightier than the sound post? Let me explain. The sound post can make the bass sound brighter or darker, depending on its placement in the bass, and balance the volume of the four strings. And that is all. Recently I have experimented with various woods for endpins and have discovered that different woods can produce different degrees of loudness in the bass. But, more importantly, they can produce different qualities of sound! By carrying several different types of wooden endpins you can change the type of sound the bass produces at will. It is like carrying different basses in one gig bag!

Several months ago my colleague Bill Merchant gave me a length of 5/8th inch carbon fiber rod. This made the bass louder than the wooden endpin then in the bass, but the sound was coarse and unpleasant. It then occurred to me that if this change in material could make such a difference in the sound, what would different types of wood produce? I acquired 5/8th inch rods of maple, hickory, cherry, oak, mahogany, and black walnut, in addition to the carbon fiber rod I already had.

I discovered that not only did each wood produce a distinct amount of sound, but each also produced a different quality of sound. Maple produced more volume of sound than metal, but generally less than the other woods. Hickory was a slight improvement in volume. Cherry was even slightly better. Mahogany was a distinct improvement over the others and produced a very warm pleasant sound. But most of the time black walnut was by far the winner in the production of a loud sound. It also had a pleasant warm sound. But for bowing oak was the best because it had not only a loud sound but it produced one of the cleanest clearest sounds I have ever heard from a bowed bass. This wood would make an excellent endpin for solo classical bass playing.

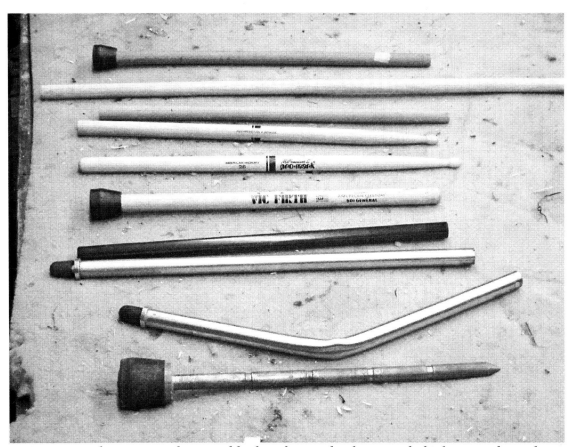

Various endpins, top to bottom- black walnut, ash, cherry, oak, hickory, rock maple, carbon fiber, straight hollow metal rod, bent hollow rod, & 10 mm. solid metal pin.

But there is more. During the course of my testing with various basses ranging in quality from doggy to excellent I discovered something else very interesting. Black walnut was mostly the winner with every bass, but on one particular bass, instead of being noticeably louder than the other woods, it was almost double the loudness of the other woods. This got me thinking that there must be something else operating to change the volume of the bass besides the stiffness and density of the various woods. Why did it make such a large difference in this particular bass?

It wasn't until Bill Merchant brought me a bass to test, that turned everything upside down, that I figured it out. This bass was an old German flat back heavy in wood. In this particular instrument black walnut did not fare well at all. Instead, it was the woods at the bottom end of the line that produced the loudest and best sound. Maple, which had produced the least increase in volume compared to the other woods when tested in all the other basses, was a clear winner with hickory not far behind.

Then I realized that I was dealing with a phenomenon called impedance matching, which was also affecting the response of the basses. If I tell you how I discovered impedance matching you will understand what it is.

Quite a few years ago I had a very good sounding Kay plywood bass in my shop for some minor repairs. It had the standard factory inserted hardwood sound post in it. I thought if this bass can sound this good with a hardwood sound post, what will it sound like with a really good one of spruce? So I made one, fitted it properly, inserted it, and the bass died. I put the original hardwood post back in and the bass came back to life. Carleen Hutchins told me I had matched the impedance of the sound post with the impedance of the bass. Plywood is stiffer than spruce and maple. Hardwood is stiffer than spruce. But put together, the two stiffnesses form an excellent marriage.

The word 'impedance' is borrowed from electrical engineering. But, whereas resistance has a fixed value which never changes, the value of impedance changes with various different factors. With basses these factors are: the design and size of the instrument; the materials used in construction; the volume of the enclosed air space; the shape and size of the F hole apertures; and the care in construction.

In basses the impedance produced by these factors is a combination of vibrating frequency, partial reflection of this frequency, and phase relationships. But when you match the impedance of the endpin with the impedance of the bass they reinforce each other and produce a louder sound in the bass.

I would like to try many other woods to see what happens; for example, teak and other Asian woods. But you can do your own experimenting. In my experiments I used a Teller model endpin available from Metropolitan Music Company, Mountain road, PO Box 1415, Stowe, Vermont; Phone: 866 846 5461, Fax: 802 253 9834. This can take a 5/8th inch (15 mm.) wooden pin. Unfortunately this type of endpin tends to slip occasionally, but a small notch cut into the wood or a small hose clamp cures this problem.

If you use a non-adjustable wooden pin that fits into a tapered shank make sure the taper of the endpin exactly fits the taper of the shank, otherwise it may rattle and you may also lose sound. Do not use wood thicker than three quarters of an inch (19 mm.) in diameter.

14

It will be too thick to vibrate properly. Even three quarter inch rods vibrate at less than optimum level. So, if possible change to the adjustable rod model with its five eighths inch endpin, which does vibrate at optimum level. Your bass will sound the better for it. However, if the adjustable endpin is longer than about eight to ten inches (25 m.) you will have to go with a thicker wood, as the thinner wood may break at such a long length.

To start your experiment you might try just maple, black walnut, and oak first rather than going out and buying a lot of different woods. You can do this later if you like. However, do not buy ebony or rosewood. They are so stiff that they are brittle and tend to crack easily. You will find the wood, or woods, that suit your bass the best, and will improve the sound. Enjoy having two or three different sounding basses in your gig bag. It will be rewarding and fun, and you will discover the endpin is mightier than the sound post.

I was going to list various woods and their specific gravities as an aid in trying various woods. The higher the specific gravity, the stiffer and harder the wood is. Maple, for example ranges in specific gravity from .44 to .56. Ebony's specific gravity ranges from .90 to 1.20. The harder the wood the brighter and generally the louder the sound is. But I decided against this listing because the element of impedance matching sometimes skews things all around. Occasionally a softer wood will produce a better sound for a certain bass better than any other wood. You will just have to experiment with your particular bass.

At the suggestion of Carleen Hutchins I tested these endpins on a variety of floorings – wood, concrete, and slate – to determine if the floor had any influence on the quality and quantity of sound that the different woods produced. It did not.

One after thought: it occurs to me that different woods in the neck will also improve sound, but this is an impractical experiment because each bass is different, and it is too costly to make half a dozen different necks to experiment with – but it is an intriguing idea.

This bass was made by John Frederick Lott in London, as labeled.

Chapter 3

The Heart and Soul of the Bass
Or
How to Make the Bass Louder and More Responsive

The most sensitive and most acoustically active part of the top of the bass lies between the F holes. By acoustically active I mean that the top is vibrating and moving in many complex ways when the bass is being played. And the most sensitive and active part of the top between the F holes lies in a little triangle drawn between the bridge feet and the sound post. The proof of this is that by moving the feet of the bridge or the sound post only a little bit we can change the volume of the bass, the feel of the bass as to whether it is easy or stiff to play, the color of the sound, and the balance of the volume between the high and low strings. A bridge that is tipped forward so that only the front edges of the bridge feet are in contact with the top is acoustically equivalent to moving the bridge forward producing undesirable sound results.

In any hand carved bass that is properly graduated the wood of the top between the F holes is thicker than at any other part of the top. With a plywood bass this is not so because the plies present an even thickness overall. However, if we add an overall patch about the size of the palm of my hand (I do not have long fingers) to the underside of the top under the bridge feet and over the sound post we can change the sound of the plywood bass from unfocused with little punch into a pretty decent sounding instrument. See Chapter 38 in my first book.

That is why this part of the top is so important to the overall sound of the bass.

The Italian word for sound post is the same as their word for soul - *l'anima*. And it can be said, without stretching reality too far, that the sound post is indeed the soul of the bass. Without it the instrument sounds exactly like what it is - a hollow box. But if this is the soul of the instrument, what is the heart?

Draw an imaginary line on the front of the bass at the fingerboard - facing side of the bridge connecting the outside edges of the bridge feet. Next draw a line from the ends of your first line to the center of the back edge of the sound post. You now have drawn a triangle. This is the heart of the bass because it is the very first part of the top to receive the vibrations of the strings, which have been transmitted there by the bridge.

It is from there that the string vibrations are transmitted to the farthest parts of the instrument at about 6000 miles per hour. It is just like a human heart pumping blood to the extremities of the body. The human heart pumps. The bass heart vibrates.

By doing something positive to the soul and to the heart separately we can make the bass louder and sustain longer - in other words, more responsive to the vibrations of the strings. By doing something to both, the increase in responsiveness will be dramatic.

When we fit the feet of a bridge to the top we try to make that fit as accurately as possible. When we fit the top of the sound post to the inside top of the bass we try to make that fit as accurately as possible. Having done so we feel we have done a very good job. But the better we make these fits the more they act to dampen the vibrations of that part of the top I have called the heart of the bass. This is because the better they fit the more bearing surface they present to the top, and it is this bearing surface which acts to dampen the motion of the top. This results in a loss of potential sound. The rest of this chapter gives an explanation of what we can do to overcome this problem and why doing so produces a positive impact on the sound of the bass.

The discovery for doing something positive for the heart was the result of taking three apparently disparate events and putting them together into one logical whole. The first was the accidental discovery that a sound post (soul) with rounded ends produced a louder sound in the bass than a regular fitted post. See Chapter 9 in my first book. The second was the viewing of a rheological (rheologey is the study of the distortion of shapes) diagram of a violin being played. The third was the memory of a man whom Ron Carter brought to my shop about twenty years ago, and who brought with him various strips of Teflon. The strips were placed under the feet of the bridge with a consequent improvement in response. The man believed this was because he had helped in fitting the bridge feet more closely to the top.

Let me start with the first event. Several years ago I had a bass in for repair before being sold. The bass had a very good sound despite several seams being open as well as several open cracks in the top. During the repairs the sound post fell down. I looked at it and was shocked to find that the ends of the post had been rounded and a small carpet tack driven into the center of the ends. I thought that if the bass sounded this good with this horrible sound post in it, what would it sound like with a properly fitted post? I made the post, inserted it into the bass in the proper place, and the sound died. I removed the tacks from the old post, inserted it and the sound returned immediately. I was shocked.

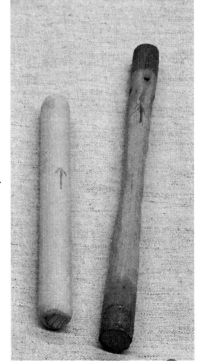

I called Carleen Hutchins, doyenne of violin acousticians, and started to tell her my story. As soon as I told her that I had replaced the terrible sound post with a good one she interrupted and ended my sentence with, "And the sound died." She then explained that the post underwent a twisting motion between the top and the back when the bass was being played. Decreasing the bearing areas of the post on the top and the back by rounding the ends had allowed the twisting motion of the top to occur more freely resulting in a louder sound. It was obvious the top was moving in at least one plane, and I was increasing the ability of the top to do this more easily. I now partially round my posts leaving a 5/8th inch flat bearing area in the center, much like the end of a drumstick, *as pictured at the right.*

But what are we doing to this heart? We fit the bridge feet as closely to the curve of the top and fit the sound post as closely as possible to the surface of the top and the back. By doing this we put as much bearing surface of bridge and sound post wood on this vibrating heart as possible. What does this do? Right! It clamps down on this wooden heart as much as possible and makes it more difficult for the heart to vibrate. It does not stop the heart from vibrating. It just makes it harder to do so. The vibrations are still there, only they are not as strong as they could be, resulting in a loss of volume in the bass. I said "…as strong as they could be." This implies that they can be made stronger. But how can it be done?

I remembered that about 20 years ago Ron Carter had brought a man into my shop who claimed he had invented a way of making the bridge fit the top more accurately and in so doing had increased the response of the bass. He had brought two kinds of thin Teflon material. One had a hard finish while the other was as pliable as a handkerchief. He had also brought several thicknesses of each. I cut pads of each of these materials to fit between the bridge feet and the top. They all increased the volume of the bass, but the one that was best was the pliable Teflon of .008 of an inch in thickness. This not only increased the volume of the bass considerably, but it also lengthened its sustain! He said he was going to patent this, and that was the last I ever heard of him. I ran out of the sample he had left, was unable to contact him, and finally forgot about the whole thing.

We thought at the time that what had happened was that the pads made the bridge fit the top more accurately. That is why the sound was louder because we were helping the bridge. Carleen Hutchins said she could improve the sound by rounding the underside of the feet slightly in the long direction of the feet. However, she didn't recommend it because cosmetically it looked like badly fitted feet. This is when I first began to suspect that the help-the-bridge theory was flawed because you shouldn't get a better response from poorly fitted feet as perfectly fitted feet.

Then one day I saw a diagram of a rheological model of a vibrating violin. The diagram consisted of little squares all connected to each other in the general shape of a violin. But the violin itself was bent and twisted and distorted in three planes to show exaggerated movements of the various parts of the instrument as it was being played. On closer look I could see that every little square had been slightly bent out of shape to accommodate the distortion of the violin.

Then I had an epiphany. If decreasing the bearing area of the sound post against the underside of the heart produced a positive result why shouldn't decreasing the bearing area of the bridge feet against the topside of the heart produce an equally positive result? And that is exactly what Carleen was doing when she rounded the feet of the bridge. By slightly rounding the feet she was decreasing the bearing area of the feet against the top. It wasn't the bridge that was being helped by the Teflon. It was the top! But how?

From the rheological sketch I could see that when the bass was being played the top was vibrating (moving) in three planes. Let me give you a simple explanation of three planes. Hold your hand in front of you with the palm down and parallel to the floor. Now move your hand away from you and back to you keeping the palm parallel to the floor. That is one plane or direction in which movement can occur. Now move your hand right and left. That is another plane. Moving your hand up and down is the third plane. But the top moves in more complex ways. It forms twists and cups and other compound distortions.

I began to experiment. I used a hard finish .008 Teflon first. It helped a little because being slippery it allowed the top to move back and forth and left and right. But because it was hard it didn't allow up and down movement. I next tried the .005 thick soft expanded PTFE Teflon. The result was better. But it was not until I tried the .008 thick soft expanded PTFE Teflon that I really got good results. The .005 wasn't thick enough to absorb all the up and down motion. The .008 was. This thickness of Teflon allowed the top to move (vibrate) more easily in all three planes producing a louder sound. I tried doubling the .005 thickness to get .01 inch thickness, but this didn't work because it was now so thick that it acted like a blanket between the bridge and the top, and impeded the ability of the bridge to communicate the string vibrations to the top.

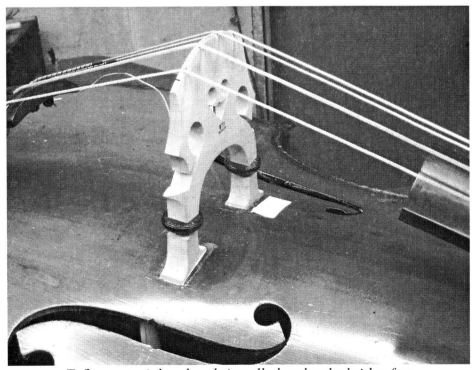

Teflon material and pads installed under the bridge feet.

I did a final test to determine once and for all if it were the bridge or the top being helped. Ned Steinberger and David Gage invented an electronic bass pickup consisting of two thin piezoelectric crystals in between two thin sheets of copper. This goes under the E foot of the bridge. I placed one Teflon pad under the G foot of the bridge and another directly between the E foot and the pickup. There was some improvement of sound. But when I took the same Teflon pad, removed it from between the pickup and the bridge foot, and placed it against the top under the pickup, the improvement in sound was dramatic. If the pad were helping the bridge the sound would immediately have been noticeably louder when the pad was placed between the pickup and the bridge foot. It was not. It was only when I placed the pad directly on the top that this happened. The top was being helped not the bridge! The Teflon was helping the top to vibrate closer to optimum level by allowing a greater freedom of movement of the top directly under the bridge feet.

What you want to order is called expanded PTFE Teflon eight thousandths (.008) of an inch thick. These are available from

      Metropolitan Music, 4861 Mountain Road, Stowe VT 05672
      sales@metmusic.com   866 846-5461

I also acquired a piece of hard finish Teflon .008 of an inch thick and a piece of expanded PTFE .005 of an inch thick elsewhere.

The Teflon placed between the bridge feet and the top reduces the damping effect of well-fitted bridge feet. What the Teflon does to that part of the top under the feet is to allow the vibrations there to have a larger excursion (amplitude). The larger excursion of the vibrations at the point where they originate, the larger and stronger will be the vibrations throughout the rest of the instrument – louder sound. The larger and stronger the vibrations are, the longer it will take them to die out (decay) – longer sustain. Put your fingers on the paper cone of a speaker. Turn the volume down to low and the paper will hardly move. Turn the volume up to high and the greater excursion of the paper produces a louder sound. A warmer sound is produced because the increased freedom of the top to vibrate means the longer wave of the lower frequencies is allowed to develop. Furthermore, I suspect that the Teflon may exert a slight damping affect on the highs adding to the warmer sound. This effect can vary from slight to noticeable, depending on the bass.

Unfortunately, this effect is subject to a diminishing return. What the Teflon is doing is helping the top to come closer to optimum vibrating level. This Teflon treatment works best on medium grade instruments. The better the instrument, the less dramatic the improvement will be because the top is already closer to optimum vibrating level. The closer the top already is to optimum vibrating level, the less improvement you will hear.

I once installed these pads on an old, very fine Italian bass brought to me by Bill Merchant, and they had a negative impact on the quality and quantity of the sound. Then I realized what had happened. Optimum and maximum are not equally interchangeable. The wood under the feet of the Italian bass was already vibrating at an optimum level. When I installed the Teflon I went beyond optimum to maximum vibrating level with a deleterious effect on the bass because the vibrating level no longer reinforced the vibrating levels of its neighbors, it conflicted with them. I had gone beyond the peak of the vibration bell curve to its downside. There can be too much of a good thing.

Try rounding the sound post ends as well as inserting the Teflon pads. You will be pleasantly surprised.

Chapter 4

Simplifying Mode Matching

In my first book I spent quite a few pages on Mode Matching. Here I am going to try to simplify things.

When things vibrate they produce a certain note. If you tap a xylophone block you will get a note. That note is the 'mode' of vibration of that particular thing. There are only four things in a bass that produce an individual note in which we are interested. If we can make any two of these four things match – or at least an exact octave apart – the bass will sound immediately louder because they are reinforcing each other.

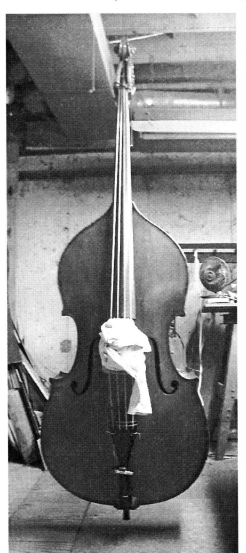

One of these four things is the note of the tailpiece when tapped. The other three notes have names. They are called A0, B0, and W'. A stands for air, B stands for body, And W' stands for wood. The little apostrophe above the W signifies that W' stands for Wood Prime. It is called Prime because it is the lowest or prime note that the wood of the bass produces. It is also the loudest note on the bass when played.

A0 – A zero – is the lowest of a series of notes (resonant frequencies) produced by the enclosed air inside the bass. The other higher notes are called A1, A2, and so on.

B0 – B zero – is the lowest of a series of notes produced by the body of the bass. There are higher body notes called B1, B2, and so on.

But how do we find these notes? Let us start with B0. Attach a cord to something strong in the ceiling. Make the cord long enough so that it reaches your chest. Adjust the endpin to its maximum length out of the bass. Now tie the cord to the neck of the bass at the nut (where there is a nodal point) so that there is no slack in the cord. Push the endpin in so that the bass is hanging unsupported in the air. Take a cloth and wrap it around the strings between the end of the fingerboard and the bridge so that when you try to play the strings, all you hear is a thud, not a note *(as pictured on left)*. But leave the fingerboard and the tailpiece free to vibrate. Now tap the end of the fingerboard. It will produce a note. At first it may be hard to distinguish a note from a thud, but keep trying.

David Brownell has had success tapping the fingerboard about a fourth of the way up the free end of the board. Also tap the top of the scroll, or the ears of the scroll. You will get the same note. The entire neck/fingerboard will vibrate as a composite unit driven by a tap at either end of the unit. Keep trying until you are certain of the pitch of the note. If you cannot get a clear note, this may be a clue that either the fingerboard or the neck (or both) are not securely glued. Check to see (and re-glue them before continuing). Now write this note down for later use.

While the bass is still hanging try to get the note of the tailpiece. Dampen the strings between the bridge and the tailpiece either with your fingers or a cloth. Now tap the tailpiece near its center. Keep trying until you are certain of the note then write it down. You now have two notes.

A0 is a little harder to find. You need a sine wave generator with its output sent to a small amplifier with a speaker small enough to fit into the bass thru the F hole. Start by holding the speaker close to the E string F hole. Then sweep slowly with your sine wave generator for one octave. At a certain pitch the note will sound noticeably louder than the other notes. Sometimes it happens that there is more than one note that sounds louder. The one that sounds the loudest is probably A0.

There are three ways to test if this note is A0. First, sounding this note, tie a string onto the speaker and lower it into the bass until it hits the bottom of the bass. Now slowly pull the speaker back out. If the note is A0 it will get louder as it reaches the F hole because the air that is being excited by this note is just between the F holes. This air does not vibrate at the ends of the bass. If it is no louder it is not A0. The second way to test if you have found A0 is to cover the G string F hole completely and try again. If this produces a lower note you have found A0.

The third way involves more equipment. This method was given to me by my good friend, colleague and excellent forward thinking repairman, Robert Branstetter of Shawnee Mission, Kansas. He uses what he calls a 'mode sniffer'. It consists of a Radio Shack analog sound level meter fitted with an adapter and a tube small enough to get thru an F hole. The adapter is made from spruce with a hole in one end to fit across the microphone end of the volume meter and a smaller hole thru the other end to hold a ½ inch PVC pipe. I prefer something more flexible. This rig measures sound levels at quite specific locations with little pickup of surrounding sound.

Insert the tube thru the G string F hole. Use the 120 setting on the volume level and the slow setting for the sensitivity. Adjust the amplifier power level so that the needle on the Radio Shack volume meter does not exceed the maximum value. Insert the speaker in the E string F hole and sweep slowly from 40 Hz to 100 Hz. The point where the volume meter reads the highest volume is A0.This is the most exact method of finding A0. Write it down.

This is the way to find W'. Place the bass on your workbench. Put your hands on the ribs just beyond the endpin block and the neck block. Sing into the E string F hole for an octave, raising or lowering the note you are singing a half tone at a time. As you get close to W' the ribs will start to vibrate under your hands. The note at which the ribs vibrate the most is W'. Write it down.

You now have four notes. The notes of A0 and W' cannot be changed, which makes things easier. The notes of B0 and the tailpiece can.

You can lower the note of the tailpiece by lengthening the tailpiece wire, adding fishing weights underneath the tailpiece, adding Plasticene (non hardening modeling clay) or plumber's epoxy putty, or by using a heavier tailpiece. Or you can try to add small clamps to the tailpiece. You can raise the note of the tailpiece by using a shorter wire, or by using a lighter tailpiece, or by removing wood from the under side of the tailpiece. You can also go to a smaller size tailpiece or a modern composite plastic tailpiece.

You can lower the note of B0 by dressing the fingerboard or neck wood thinner, by adding fishing weights underneath the end of the fingerboard, or by using heavier tuning machines. You can raise the note by using lighter tuning machines with plastic or wood spindles, or by shortening the fingerboard (be careful here), or by removing wood from the underside of the end of the fingerboard.

You cannot alter a note by more than two, or at the most, three semitones. Look at the notes you wrote down. If there are two notes within that range, at least one of which can be changed, you can match them. Outside that range, don't waste your time.

The match producing the greatest improvement in sound is B0-A0. The next best is B0-tailpiece. It is the easiest because both notes can be changed. Don't match three modes. It doesn't work. At this writing nobody knows why. Other possible matches are- B0-W', tailpiece-W', and tailpiece-A0. Check to see if A0-W' is an accidental match.

Adding weight produces a darker sound suitable for arco work. Lightening things produces a brighter sound more suitable for pizzicato playing.

Don't shorten the tailpiece wire to the point where there is less than 1 inch of wire between the tailpiece and the saddle. Doing so will make the tailpiece so rigid it will not vibrate properly and will kill the sound of the bass. Don't lengthen the wire to the point where the distance of the E string between the tailpiece and the bridge is less than 6 ¾ inches (171mm). It will kill the sound of the E string.

If you change strings and had a match involving the tailpiece, check that it still matches. Different strings have different tensions which will change the note of the tailpiece. Also check BO. There may be a change here, although it will be much less than the tailpiece change because of the much greater mass of the neck/fingerboard compared to the match of the tailpiece.

Don't be afraid to try, and good luck.

Chapter 5

Making a Bass Brighter or Darker

Lately I have been corresponding by phone with an up and coming bass specialist who is having great success using my "less-is-more" methods of repair. He recently restored a bass for an out of town client. When it was done the bass had a sound big enough to fill a house. The owner came in when the bass was done, played a few notes, paid his bill and hurried back home. A few days later the repairman got a call from the owner saying that he was dissatisfied with the bass because it sounded too dark. I advised the repairman that rather than have a customer badmouthing him, to tell the customer that he would pay to have the bass shipped back to him and he would make it brighter sounding. I then sent the repairman a copy of this chapter.

When the bass arrived he unpacked it and was shocked to find that the customer had installed a set of very dark sounding strings. As far as I can tell, the customer never realized that you can change the sound of a bass merely by changing the type of strings you install. So before you do any of the things listed below make sure you have the best type of strings for the sound you want. Then if that isn't enough try the remedies listed here.

Everything that is listed here can be found in my first book, *The Setup and Repair of the Double Bass for Optimum Sound,* but the information is scattered about in several different chapters making it hard to find, so I have gathered it all here in one place for easier access.

I will start with making a bass sound brighter because it is easier to do than making it sound darker.

1) The lighter the tailpiece the brighter the sound. This is because if we lower the mass of the tailpiece while keeping everything else the same, it then raises the note (the modal Hz) of the entire tailpiece assembly, as would shortening the loop of the hanger wire. Try a ¼ or ½ size tailpiece. Get a plastic one or one made of white wood stained black because they are lighter than ebony. Be prepared to try both. It may alter a Mode Match, but do the best you can.

2) Insert a 5/8th inch (16mm) sound post. In rare occasions a hardwood post will help. Try using a spruce post with a closer grain first. If this isn't enough help use a hardware store bought birch dowel. It will do as well as anything.

3) Thin the bridge by removing wood from the fingerboard facing front of the bridge. Do not thin from the back side because this is the side which is used to determine the angle at which the bridge is fitted to the top. Do not thin the top edge less than 3 mm and the bottom feet less than 5/8ths of an inch (11 mm) front to back. If you do you will lose volume. These are absolutely minimum dimensions.

4) Move the sound post closer to the foot of the bridge, but do not go too close as this will kill the sound and make the bass stiff and harder to play.

5) Move the bridge and the post closer to the fingerboard. Do not go more than ¼ of an inch (6mm) as this will move the bridge out of the heart of the sound and will kill the sound and make the bass stiff and harder to play. Try 1/8th of an inch (3mm) closer.

6) Use brighter strings. The Pirastro Eudoxa is an example of a very dark string. Try Thomastik Spirocore, or Pirastro Obligato.

To make a bass darker do the following things-

1) Try darker sounding strings such as Pirastro Eudoxa or Thomastik Superflexible. The type of string you use can make a big difference in the quality of the sound.

2) Either get a very heavy tailpiece, or better, add lead fish weights, testing first as to the amount of weight, to the underside of the tailpiece. The lowest note on a xylophone is always the longest heaviest block of wood. If you use a big heavy tailpiece do not make the tailpiece wire less than 1 inch (25 mm.) in length between the saddle and the tailpiece as this will make the tailpiece too rigid to vibrate properly. And do not make the string distance between the tailpiece and the bridge less than 6 ¾ inches (171 mm.) as this will kill the sound of the E string **but** do not change anything if there is an existing mode match.

3) If the present bridge thickness from face to face measures less than 6 mm. at the top edge and 1 inch (25 mm.) at the feet front to back, make a new one with these dimensions.

4) Move the sound post further away from the bridge foot.

5) Move the bridge and the sound post further away from the fingerboard, but do not move it more than for making the bass brighter as above.

6) Get a piece of wide grain pine and make a post as large as will fit into the bass through the bottom eye of the F hole. Round the top and bottom of the post so that there is a ¾ inch bearing area on both ends.

Chapter 6

More About Sound Posts

I was just about to deliver some profound thoughts on sound posts when here you come running to tell me your bass has just suffered a disaster. I am thinking about a crushed top or a broken neck when you tell me the sound post has fallen and is rolling around inside the bass and you have a gig that night. "What to do, watodo, watodo?"

The first thing to do is get the post out of the bass. I leave that entirely up to you. But once out we have to figure out a way to get it back in. Loosen the bass strings about four or five turns to prevent the bridge from pushing the top in. If the post won't jam loosely into position when you try to install it you will have to tighten the strings again. The tried and true way to do this is to get a long string and tie the post about in the middle of the string just about an inch below the top of the post.

But there you are standing holding a piece of kindling in your hand, and you don't know which is what. Every post has some geography attached to it. There is a top and a bottom and a front and a back. Almost every post has a small notch in one side. This notch is always closer to the top of the post than the bottom, and it is on the side facing the F hole. Sometimes a pencil line on the post will tell you the same thing. So that takes care of that.

Try to line this notch up with the bass G string end of the string because this is the side of the post that should face the F hole. Get another string and tie the post in the same way about an inch above the bottom of the post. Now take some Scotch tape and fasten one end of the two strings together. Put this end into the bass from the G string side F hole and push it toward the opposite F hole. Snake this taped end out of the E string F hole with whatever you can find to do it with, and remove the tape.

Now pull the ends of the string attached to the top of the post taut. The post will start to stand up. Keep pulling this string back and forth until the edge of the post facing the bridge foot sits about ½ inch (13mm) behind the back edge of the G string foot and the center of the post is about opposite the center of the foot. Now pull the top of the post a tad closer to the F hole. Hopefully the notch in the post is facing more or less toward the F hole.

This, by the way, is the spot you set up a sound post for the first time before you start moving it to change the color of the sound between bright and dark and the volume balance of the strings between the low ones and the high ones. If the post falls down you will have to tighten the bass strings back up again. Then start pulling the ends of the string attached to the bottom of the post until the post is more or less vertical. That is about the best you can do, but it will get you through the night until you can get to a repairer to do it right. Now just throw the string ends back into the bass until you can get to that repairer. They won't harm the sound at all.

The closer the post is to the bridge foot, the brighter the tone and vice versa. The closer the post is to the F hole the louder the E and A strings will be compared to the other two and vice versa.

But in my first book, *The Setup and Repair of the Double Bass for Optimum Sound*, I gave instructions on how to make and position a sound post. However, there are other things about them that I did not mention.

There are some rules about sound posts that I would like to give you. A harder wood will give a brighter sound; a softer wood, a darker sound. There are practical limits to this. A very hard post, such as one made of ebony, will decrease the volume of the bass because it is just too hard to vibrate properly. If you could make a post out of balsa wood it would do the same thing because the wood is so soft it would absorb vibrations. The softest wood I have been able to use is very wide grain pine. I will explain more of this later. The denser the wood is, the brighter the sound will be, within limits, and vice-versa.

The smaller the diameter of the post the brighter the sound will be because the post has less bearing surface against the top allowing the shorter wave length vibrations to develop; the larger the diameter the darker the sound. Again, there are practical limits to this. The smallest practical diameter is 5/8ths of an inch (16 mm.). Any less than this will cause a bump in the top directly over the post. The biggest practical diameter is 7/8ths of an inch (22 mm.). Anything larger than this will impede the ability of the top to vibrate properly, with a consequent loss of sound.

I recently restored a bass which, when finished, had a dark, round sound. I realized that this sound character could not be changed no matter what I did. So I decided to enhance this dark warm sound and make it into an even nicer sounding bass for arco work. I used the two rules I just wrote about – a very soft wood of a large diameter. I found a piece of very wide grain soft pine, and I made it into a post with a 15/16ths of an inch (24 mm.) diameter. I was just able to get this into the bass through the lower eye of the F hole. Once fitted and positioned the large diameter choked the sound of the instrument. But I rounded the ends of this post, as mentioned in my book, down to the point where there was only 3/4ths of an inch (19 mm.) of post wood actually touching the top and back. This had the desired result, and gave the bass an even darker, warmer sound than a conventional spruce post.

But a thought has recently occurred to me. If different woods in the endpin can make a noticeable difference in the quality and quantity of the sound of the bass, what could different woods in the sound post do? I have not had either the time or the opportunity to test out this idea, so it is something I leave for you to do. Who knows what you may discover! Exciting, isn't it?

In my first book I recommended that the post be vertical. This may not be the best position for a particular bass. I have learned that the position of the bottom of the post is as important to the sound of the bass as the position of the top. This may lead to a position for the post that is somewhat tilted in the bass. For example, you may have found that no matter what you did with the top of the post the volume of the E and A was less than that of the D and G. If you move the bottom of the post closer to the center of the bass you will find that you have increased the volume of the E and A to the point where the overall volume of the four strings may well be balanced.

But now the post doesn't fit as well as it did before this tilting. Refit the top of the post so that it doesn't make a dent in the underside of the top, but you can leave the bottom alone. Years ago George Mraz brought in his bass for some minor work. While doing this I noticed his post had been moved so that the top no longer fitted against the top of the bass. I reset to post so that it fitted, and the sound died. I put it back where it had been, and the sound returned. This happened for the same reason that rounding the ends of a post will increase the volume of sound. The post undergoes a twisting motion when the bass is being played, and the less that motion is impeded by placing less post bearing surface against the top and back the louder the sound will be. So don't worry if the post no longer fits properly.

So, just as a matter of curiosity, try moving the bottom of the post around, north and south, east and west, to see what happens. You may be surprised, and you may learn something. Moving the post no more than 1/8th of an inch (3 mm) will be sufficient to change things. But move the top and bottom of the post until you get exactly what you want. Have fun experimenting.

One final observation: if the post has been down for awhile before you reinstall it, the sound of the bass will change slightly overnight.

An interesting violin shaped bass made by Barbe pere, as stamped.

Chapter 7

Strings

David Brownell, one of the coauthors of my first book, suggested I do a chapter on strings because the kind of strings you use can alter the type of sound and the amount that the bass produces. At first, I thought this was a good idea, but I soon realized that I just didn't have enough information to write about this subject knowledgeably. I now do only minor adjustments for my friends so I do not have access to the opinions of the scores of players who used to come into my shop in New York City.

Then Robert Kopec, my very good friend and excellent young bass player, told me about two web sites on the internet where bass players can get information on strings without having to go to the considerable expense of buying different sets of strings and experimenting. I will give you this information later.

First, let me give you a rather short and incomplete history of strings and how they evolved to their present state. In the beginning, when the bass viol (not violin) first began to develop, the bass had four strings. In order for the bottom string to have enough mass to play the low notes it was made so thick that it almost became a small rope. Players began to discard it. The most expensive part of the bass was the tuning machines and makers soon learned to install only three machines.

Then, as the literature developed, composers began to write for lower bass notes. Wagner, in fact, wrote for low C, hence the necessity for a C extension. The bass changed from three to four strings, generally, but not always, tuned from the bottom E. A. D, G. However, the gut E string was still so thick that it was unwieldy to play. The string makers found they could overcome the problem of mass by wrapping the gut E and A strings in thin silver coated copper wire, and did so.

About the middle of the 20th century two things began to happen to shape the course of string making. Symphony orchestras began to ask for more clarity from the bass section, and pizzicato players began to ask for more volume. For a short while these needs were met by plastic coated gut strings such as Red-O-Ray. But these two goals were better served by the introduction of metal strings.

Gradually, over the years, a growing number of pizzicato players found that most of the steel strings available to them were too metallic sounding (such as Thomastik Spirocore) or too 'thumpy' (such as Pirastro Eudoxa). They yearned for the warmth of gut strings. Some of them started to go back to gut and are still playing them. But the warmth they gained was off set by the loss of volume. Recently string makers have been introducing various types of synthetic strings which are closer in sound to the warmth of gut but have not lost the volume of steel. Furthermore, they are not subject to the problems of gut strings such as constant tuning in humid weather and lack of durability.

So now we have three types of strings currently on the market – gut, steel, and synthetic. No wonder players are seeking information on the sound and playability of different brands of strings. This is where you can find it: www.talkbass.com or www.gollihurmusic.com. You can find more information there than I could possibly include in this chapter. Good luck, and enjoy.

Bill Merchant says, "I warn my clients that use the new synthetic core strings that these strings biggest short coming is that the attack you can produce on them is limited by the soft core. Players come in complaining their bass tightened up on the gig but upon examination the bass is found to be set up correctly - it sounds and plays fine at home or in the shop. But when in louder situations, in a bigger space and possibly with a loud drummer, playing the bass harder only makes their hands hurt, as the sound's attack doesn't increase like it does with the stiffer metal core pizzicato strings. Lower tension strings also require that the action be higher." He likes to say "low and tight beats high and floppy", as far as bass action is concerned. You can have lower overall action with metal core strings than with many of these gut analogs.

A bass made by James Cole, as stamped.

Chapter 8

Putting on Strings

In looking back on my career as a repairman I realized that I taught more than a few of my customers - students, big name players alike - how to put strings on a bass. My teacher, Fred Zimmerman, didn't teach me. It was my repairman who showed me how to do it correctly. That is why I am writing this chapter for you.

Don't take all the strings off at once and then proceed. If you do the bridge will move out of position and the chances that the sound post will fall down are pretty good. Do it one string at a time while all the others are in full tension.

I start with the G string. I remove the old string and save it. The only time a string breaks is when you don't have a spare. Line the hole in the spindle up so that it faces more or less up and more or less toward the nut. Insert the new string in the tailpiece. Take the loose end and put it in the hole in the spindle. When it comes out the other side pull the end of the string up and out of the tuning box.

Keep pulling the loose end of the string until there is almost no slack in the part of the string you will be playing on. However, and this is important, don't pull the string so that the metal part of the string goes into the spindle. Only the silk covered end of the string should touch the spindle, not the naked metal even though you may have to do a lot of turning to take up slack. The reason for this is that some spindle holes may have a sharp edge which will cut into the metal and later cause the string to break.

Now take the loose end of the string and pull it toward the tuning machine, whichever machine you are putting the string on. The reason you are doing this is so that the strings will lead properly into the tuning box and not cross over one another. From there take the loose end of the string and put it under that part of the string which will be in tension. Hold it taut while you tune up until that part of the string which will be in tension presses the loose end of the string up against the spindle and jams it in place. This will make sure that the new string will never slip at just the wrong time. Make sure the string is in the correct notch in the bridge and nut, and keep on tuning up until the string is in tune.

I then go to the D string. If you have done everything properly nothing will be in the way of installing this string. Next do the E string, and, finally, the A string. Don't cut off the loose ends because if the strings have to be removed for a repair it will be almost impossible to reinstall a cut string. You can leave them dangling or curl them up to suit yourself. Finally, check the bridge to make sure that in tuning up the strings it hasn't been pulled forward toward the fingerboard. If so, carefully and gently pull it back into position. I place myself at the endpin end of the bass, place both elbows on the top, and carefully and slowly shake the bridge while pulling it back toward me. This way the bridge won't suddenly pull all the way back to you and come down with a bang.

Enjoy your new strings.

Chapter 9

Things that Hurt the Sound

The previous chapters dealt with things that helped the sound. This chapter deals with things that don't.

The need for this chapter arose when Ron Carter called me recently to talk about sound. During the course of the conversation we began to talk about things that hurt the sound of the bass.

Some are quite obvious, like a bridge that has been knocked out of position or a sound post that has somehow drifted far away from its proper place. But others are not. The first sentence of **Traeger's Principle** states, "When a bass is being played everything is vibrating...." Anything done that mutes or inhibits these vibrations is deleterious to the sound. Here they are -

The notches for the strings in both the nut and the bridge sometimes get cut so deeply that the strings sit down in ditches with the wood on both sides rising up above them. This wood acts somewhat like a mute and inhibits the vibrations slightly. At most, only the bottom third of the string should sit in the notch so that the string can vibrate as freely as possible.

There are a number of pickups on the market which are attached to various parts of the bridge. Anything that is attached to the bridge adds mass to the bridge and, therefore, has a muting affect. Some pickups are attached in such a way as to actually impede the natural motion of the bridge. Again there is a loss. In my opinion the pickups that have the least negative influence on the bridge are the ones which have the pick up(s) installed in the adjuster wheels, such as the Fishman Full Circle.

The bass pictured here is Ron Carter's main bass, on which I have worked, made by Anton Schroetter in Mittenwald, Germany, as labeled.

Then we come to the tailpiece and pickup jacks. There is one which is clamped onto the A and D strings below the bridge. This begins to impede the natural motion of the tailpiece, and for Optimum Sound the tailpiece must be as free as possible to vibrate. Other jacks are attached to the tailpiece itself adding mass and inhibiting the motion of the tailpiece. Perhaps the best pickup is a goose neck mike clamped onto the side of the bass.

The combined mass of all these extras mounted on the tail piece of the bass has an adverse effect on its sound.

There are other things which have been attached to the tailpiece which impedes its natural motion with negative sound results. A lot of players attach a bow quiver to the tailpiece. This is one of the worst things you can do. Don't! Other players keep a cloth tucked between the tailpiece and the top to wipe off rosin from the top. Again, Don't!

Finally, the tailpiece hanger cable is sometimes made of solid metal like a coat hanger. This makes the tailpiece too rigid to vibrate properly. Sometimes the cable is spread so far apart over the saddle that it again makes the tailpiece too rigid to vibrate properly. This is only acceptable if it is part of a mode matching adjustment.

For Optimum Sound *everything* must be as free as possible to vibrate properly. Remember this and your bass will be the better off for it.

II - REPAIR

CHAPTERS 10 Thru 19

Chapter 10

Before Beginning a Major Repair or Overhaul

When undertaking major work on an instrument, the most important thing is to talk to your customer and ask him or her about their idea of sound. What do they like? What do they want? Make sure you fully understand their conception of sound before you begin. Carefully examine the bass so that later on there will be no necessary extra work that was not discovered during the initial examination.

Then tell them clearly and concisely that you can make red redder but you can't make red green. In other words, tell them you can bring out the most of what that particular bass has to offer, but you can't change its natural character. If it is a dark bass, you can do only so much to make it brighter, and it may never be as bright as the customer would like. The reverse is true of bright basses.

Make sure they fully understand thus point because it will avoid disappointments in the future.

David Brownell then does something I advise all repairers to do. He writes down everything that he and his client have discussed and attaches this to the bass rather than just using a baggage tag.

Write down as explicitly as possible everything that is going to be done, how it is going to be done and why. If there is a monetary constraint that prevents something being done write this down also. Write down what you can guarantee and what you can't as in the case of a neck reset in a mortise which was previously done with white glue.

Date the paper, initial it and have your customer initial it also. The reason for this is that what a person hears and what that person later remembers hearing are quite often completely dissimilar. This is your guarantee that there can be no argument when the job is finished. Then do your best to make your customer happy.

Chapter 11

A Shrunken Back Repair

I had finished writing this book. I had finished rewriting and editing the book. I had finished the sixth and last proof reading. And then I got a phone call from a general repairer in Easton, Pennsylvania.

He had just gotten in a bass that had been in a flood of some kind or other. When the bass dried out the back had shrunk so much that it had pulled the ribs in, which meant that the ribs in the top garland had pulled out. The top no longer fitted. He had my book but did not want to do a center seam inlay on a round back bass, the most difficult and expensive single repair, and the owner said he could not afford that expensive a repair anyway.

But the bass had been a good old work-horse instrument and the repairer wanted to know if there was anything else that could be done to save it. I told him that he could pull in one or both ribs and that would do the trick. And it was then that I realized that I had never described this repair in detail because it was – horror of horrors – an irreversible repair. I had alluded to it in passing in my book saying. "…this is a permanent change in the outline and interior air space of the bass…" and let it go at that.

This is the best method for pulling the rib in; the only one for violin cornered basses. Remove the top completely. You may have to do this for both ribs to get a fit but it is advisable to do one rib at a time. Separate the rib from the back from the corner block to the endpin block. Now separate the rib from the endpin block with either steam and a pallet knife or a 50-50 mixture of white vinegar and water and the same knife. Pull the rib in so that the end of the rib extends past the rib join at the block. Hold the rib in place with a couple of spool clamps and examine the fit of the rib and the back to see if you have gone beyond the point where there is a good gluing surface for the rib and back. You may have to back off the rib a bit to do this.

When you have solved the problem of the rib fit to the back get two small brad nails. Measure their thickness with a caliper and get a drill bit the same thickness. Drill two small holes in the rib about an inch from the top and the back and into the block. Now fasten the rib to the block with the brads. Just drive the brads in far enough so they won't slip. You don't want to drive them home because you will be removing them later.

Now remove the spool clamps and put the top on loosely to see if it now fits. Hopefully, it does, but if it doesn't some slight adjustment of the rib should allow the rib to have a good gluing surface for both the back and the top. Cut off the excess rib cleanly at the block, remove the excess inside linings, and glue the rib to the block. When that has set remove the brads, fill in the holes, and glue the rib to the back. When that has set put the top back on and set the bass up. You can now congratulate yourself for having saved the bass. If at some future time a center seam inlay is installed, the rib can be pulled back out and a piece of rib stock added on to the place where it had been previously removed. So in fact it is only an almost irreversible repair.

Chapter 12

Five String Neck Thicknesses

In my book I listed the optimum thicknesses for a four string bass, but failed to mention them for a five string bass.

But before I go any further I must mention a prejudice – well, maybe not a prejudice so much as an opinion formed over many years of listening to many, many basses. I have never heard a five string bass that sounded as well as a good four string version. The reason is that the neck is too wide to allow the neck/fingerboard to vibrate laterally at an optimum level compared to a four string neck. And often the neck is too thick to allow it to vibrate at an optimum level in the front to back direction. Furthermore, the nut is too wide as well as the bridge top. The extra width pushes the outside strings further apart and thus increases the lateral forces on both the neck and the bridge. These forces tend to dampen the vibrations of both the neck and the bridge, much like the stays stabilizing a cell phone tower holding it rigidly in place. Finally, there is the extra weight of a fifth tuning machine which further inhibits the motions of the neck/fingerboard.

The reason that a three string bass by Jean Plumerel, which I restored for the Metropolitan Museum of Art, sounded so good was that it had none of the inhibitory factors listed above.

This will annoy many five string bass players, but it is my opinion. However, I am willing to be proved wrong.

But to get back to neck thicknesses; they should never be less than those recommended for four string basses. The optimum thickness of the combined neck/fingerboard at the A note on the G string should be 1 ½ inches (37mm). The thickness at the D note on the G string (or as close as you can get to it before the neck curves into the neck butt) should be 1 ¾ inches (44mm). For a five string neck these thicknesses should never be exceeded by more than 1/8th of an inch (3mm) for Optimum Sound.

Chapter 13

Stand Height

In my first book, *The Setup and Repair of the Double Bass for Optimum Sound*, I recommended a stand height of no more than 1 ½ inches (38 mm.) maximum. Stand height is the distance measured at the neck butt between the top of the bass and the underside of the fingerboard. The other day Bill Merchant brought me a beautiful old Italian bass with large violin shaped shoulders.

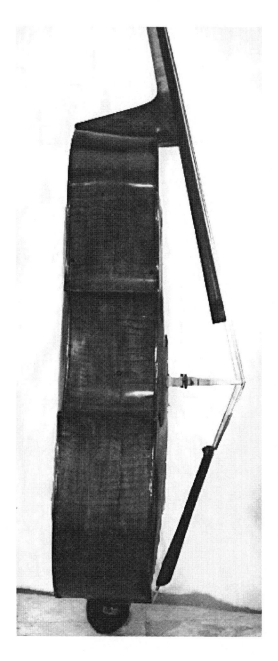

Wide shoulders on a bass generally make it a bit difficult for the player to reach the notes in the upper positions because he or she has to reach around these shoulders to get at the fingerboard.

Bill has overcome the awkwardness of playing the upper register on this particular instrument by setting the neck in with a stand height of 2 inches (51 mm.) *as pictured at the left*. This indeed overcomes the upper register problem by making the fingerboard more easily accessible and does not look unappealing. In fact, it looks quite normal.

I have decided that this is the best way to handle a bass with this type of construction, and I now recommend it to all my readers.

Some of the older basses have almost no stand height at all necessitating a very low bridge. This means that unless the strings are set very far apart on the bridge the player will hit the side of the bass at the C bout with the bow when playing. The only solution to this is to reset the neck with a proper stand height and neck angle, which will produce a higher bridge on which the string can be spaced properly. It is the stand height and the angle of the neck/fingerboard which dictates the height of the bridge. Try to reset the stand height and neck angle so that you will wind up with a bridge about 6 ¾ inches (171 mm.) high. The bass will probably sound better with a higher bridge than the original low one.

Chapter 14

Flat Back Cross Bars

In my first book I recommended thinning out the cross bars from their center to the ends, gradually making them thinner as they reached the ends so that when tapped they would produce the same note for their entire length. This thinning, unfortunately, changes B1 too much in a direction you don't want to go by lowering the pitch of B1. B1 is higher in pitch than A1. If the difference between A1 and B1 is greater than 100 Hz the bass will be harsh and unplayable.

If the difference is 40 Hz or less you will lose all 'punch' and just have a smooth and easy playing instrument. The preferable difference is between 60 Hz and 80 Hz.

Thin out the center bar so that at its center it produces the same note when tapped as the adjacent part of the back plate. However, the combined thickness of the bar and the back plate at this point should be about 3/4ths of an inch (19 mm). Anything less produces an unfocused sound. Anything more impedes the sound. Then thin out the other bars so that at their centers *only* they all produce this same note rather than gradually thinning the bar from end to end. Keep this center thickness for the entire length of the bar. If a bar is wide and flat so that its note is lower than that of the center bout bar, replace it with a thicker, less wide bar, and dress it properly. This will change B1 less, and the bass will not lose its 'punch'.

The ends of the bars should never be let into the rib linings. Allow at least ¼ of an inch (6 mm) in between the ends of the bars and the linings. This allows the back plate to vibrate more easily, producing a better and bigger sound.

In round back basses sometimes the center along the seam of the back is too thin. This makes the bass 'boom' and overshadows the notes to the point where it may make the bass difficult to play, especially in fast passages. This condition can be overcome by gluing in a center seam strap cleat running the entire length of the center seam from end to end. This cleat should be at least 1 inch (25 mm) wide and 1/8th of an inch (3 mm.) thick.

Chapter 15

Alternate Methods

Here is what I wrote in my first book. "What I have written here are my methods of doing things. That is why I have written in the first person singular, in order to emphasize this point. They sometimes may not be the best or the most traditional methods, but they work for me. Some other useful approaches are described for many of the problems. However, you may find that an entirely different approach works better for you. Use it."

Here are some alternate methods. The first is not only an alternate one, but a safer one.

Cleaning Agents

In my first book I recommended xylene as a solvent to clean caked on rosin dust from the top of a bass. We have learned that use (or misuse) of this may involve health hazards, so don't use it. In its place let me suggest a product called Simple Green™, widely available in stores in a spray bottle. It will take a little longer to work, but it will work, leaving a nice clean surface without damage to the varnish. Much safer, and it is nonflammable!

Be wary of advice in old books such as the use of carbon tetrachloride and some bleaches. These are damaging.

I mentioned in my first book that de-ionized water is also a good cleaning agent. Rubbing with a cloth will take off many stains. Just be sure not to soak too much into the varnish or wood. But de-ionized water is not stable. It will deteriorate in anywhere from two weeks to six months into ordinary water. It is available from chemical supply houses and health food stores.

Gluing Cleats

When gluing cleats I put glue on both surfaces and then wait about half a minute before clamping. Gary Rickman uses an alternate method. He puts glue on both surfaces and then waits until the glue begins to jelly. He then warms both glued surfaces with a hair dryer until the glue is liquid again and then clamps. This may be overkill, but it certainly ensures a molecular bond because of the extra time the glue has to sink into the wood.

Bass Bar Placement

In my chapter on bass bars (in my first book) I recommended placing the bar $1/7^{th}$, $1/8^{th}$, or $1/9^{th}$ of the width of the bout distant from the center seam. But half increments are also good such as 1/7.5, 1/8.5, and so on. Even quarter increments are OK. If it looks and feels right, that is what counts. Nothing is written in stone. The most important thing is to use the same increment for both the upper and lower bout measurements.

Spool Clamp Slipping

In my first book I tried to be as encyclopedic as possible, but recently I had a phone call from a repairer who was working on his first bass, which showed me I had forgotten something. He was putting a top back on when all of a sudden he ran into a problem. The bass had a 'break' in the top part of the back that was causing his spool clamps to slip. Many basses, both flat and round back, have what is called a 'break' in the upper back.

There are two kinds of backs. In the one the back is straight from end to end. In the other there is a 'break' in the back at about the middle of the upper bout where the back suddenly bends in toward the neck butt. This means that the edges of the back are no longer more or less parallel to the top edges, but instead are at an angle to them. Quite frequently the bottom of the spool clamp begins to slide up to the neck butt instead of remaining in place.

The cure for clamp slippage is to take a piece of 120 weight sandpaper about 1 inch wide and 2 inches long. Fold it in two so that the sandpaper side is out, and place this between the bottom of the spool clamp and the back edge. Generally this will stop the bottom of the clamp from sliding. Do not use 80 weight sandpaper as it will scratch the varnish. If the sandpaper slides on itself just change the angle at which you inserted it. If you have used pieces of sandpaper use one of them instead of a new piece. If the sandpaper leaves scratches, these can be removed by putting some linseed oil on a cloth and then adding alcohol drop by drop and trying it each time on the affected area. Eventually you will feel the varnish begin to gel slightly. Rub slightly and the scratches will disappear.

However, David Brownell has developed a different technique. He fits some of his spool clamps with suede or smooth Naugahide. These materials are much less likely to slip. He also makes the hole in the bottom spool larger so that it will conform to the angle of the back. Good idea.

Cleat Steamer

When removing old cleats and old glue I used a flask with a long rubber hose to steam off the old glue. Gary Rickman tried this for a while until he dropped the flask and broke it. So he went out and bought himself a wallpaper steamer, adapted the nozzle to make a smaller hole for the steam to escape, and was back in business with a different product to produce directed steam and one that was practically unbreakable.

If you have to remove a cross bar or big chunks of ebony still glued to a neck from which you have just removed the fingerboard, I prefer to cut them down with a wide mouth gouge and then plane off the rest until just a paper thin piece of wood is left to be steamed off. This method uses less steam than any other I can think of and therefore there is less moisture absorption by the wood.

Positioning Ribs

Sometimes when you go to put a top back on there will be places in the ribs which have bent inward and no longer fit the top. I used to push these places out with a long bent metal rod. And if this didn't work I would install a wood dowel between the ribs, with a string on it for subsequent removal, to push out the offending rib back into place. But this same repairman took a cheap butter knife, bent the tip at a ninety degree angle, inserted it in between the top and the rib, and pulled the rib out. Just before he installed the last spool clamp he could pull the knife out and the rib would be in its proper place for gluing. This is another good and different idea.

Humidity

In my first book I spoke of the dangers of too high and too low humidity. Too low in the winter and the bass will probably crack. Too high in the summer when you are doing an overhaul or restoration and the bass will probably crack the next winter.

Gary Rickman recently had an unusual problem. A customer brought him a flat back bass that had cracked during the winter and had not been repaired. It was now summer and the wood of the back had swollen up to the point where the sides of the crack which had never been lined up were jammed so tightly together that not only could he not line them up properly but he could not get a drop of glue in to do a repair.

He solved the problem by placing a heating pad over the crack overnight. The next morning the wood had dried out sufficiently so that the crack had opened enough so that he could line up the sides and then glue.

These are some of the alternate methods I have heard about since I wrote my book. But if you don't have one, use my method. It will work.

Another view of the Eighteenth Century Italian violin shaped bass pictured on page 38.

Chapter 16

Don't Be Upset When…….

(This chapter is written for beginner repair persons or repairers who see a bass only once in a blue moon.)

….you removed a fingerboard prior to installing a new one and you discover that the neck has not only warped forward but has twisted. This is not at all uncommon.

For every problem there is a solution. The solution to this one is easy. Place the bass on your bench on its back so that the neck hangs out over the end. Put weights on the top of the bass at the endpin end of the bass. Now put a cloth on the scroll to protect it and put weights on the scroll (I use my heavy extended C clamps) until the neck is straight, or as nearly straight as you can get it. Placing most of the weight of the clamp on one side or the other will tend to straighten out a twist.

If the neck is now straight you can go ahead and glue on your fingerboard blank. If it is still curved, wet the flat surface with a damp towel and heat it with an infrared lamp. Repeat this process until the neck is straight. This may take a while, so don't be impatient. You may have to soak the neck overnight in order to straighten it. But eventually the neck will become straight.

…. you have removed rib doubling, which is the proper thing to do every time, and you discover that the ribs are now no longer flat, but instead are curved and wavy. The explanation is simple. Over the years all the blocks have shrunk lengthwise. The only way the ribs can accommodate this decrease in length is to bend and curve upon themselves. Don't worry. This won't affect the sound adversely at all. In fact the curved ribs, which are now at their original thickness, will help the bass to sound better because they are now free to vibrate properly. The proper thickness for a rib is 2 ½ mm.

Repair the cracks with an absolute minimum of cleats using linen wherever possible. The least amount of repair is the best because you don't want to stiffen up the ribs all over again.

…. you discover that the top you have just removed so slowly and carefully has left splinters of itself still attached to the rib garland. No matter how careful you are and how slowly you go this will almost inevitably happen because someone has used regular strength glue to seal a slightly open seam some time in the past. My mentor, Joseph Cillecek, said that he never let a client watch him remove a top because the client would see the splinters and complain that he was destroying the bass.

Carefully remove the splinters and glue them back onto the top. If there are still gaps in the top edge fill them in with slips of wood or other suitable filler. This not only affects the reliable gluing of the top to the ribs, but air gaps left will affect the sound, as will ragged plate wood over the end blocks that reduces the glue contact surface over the blocks leading to poor glue bonding. You can now continue with the repair which necessitated removing the top in the first place.

….you discover that the bass you have so carefully and properly restored and set up for Optimum Sound has a horrendous wolf note that it never had before. Don't be discouraged. You did the right thing. Now that the bass is able to vibrate so much more at Optimum Sound it produces a wolf note which it never did before. A wolf note is the note of the wood of the bass. If it is very close to a note being played it will 'beat' against that note as it reinforces and diminishes the volume of that note. Most fine instruments have one. Buzzes and rattles are not wolf notes. You will feel the wolf note with the bow, which will try to skip across the string and not play the intended note.

Homer Mensch had a beautiful bass attributed to Gagliano *(pictured right)* on which I have worked that had such a bad wolf note on the G flat on the D string that when he saw that note on the music in front of him he never played it, preferring to let the rest of the section do it. The bottom line is this- the better the bass and the better condition it is in, the louder the wolf note

Gary Karr's old bass, the so called Koussevitsky Amati (now thought to be Nineteenth Century French made), had a bad wolf note close to the A note (I believe) on the G string. He just babied it when he had to play it. But the rest of the bass sounded like a cannon. If you try to eliminate the wolf note you will only diminish the sound of the rest of the bass. Put up with it.

….a customer for whom you did a restoration six months ago calls you up and tells you he can see light through cracks in the ribs, and he is concerned whether this will affect

44

the sound. These cracks are always tiny and short. Tell him not to worry. It won't affect the sound. This is a not uncommon occurrence. Often a new crack will appear right beside one you just repaired. You can fix this by using a mechanical finger to lay a piece of linen about a half inch wide and no more than six inches long, which has been dipped in the glue pot and laid over the crack through the F hole. If you can't reach some of the cracks through the F hole fill them in from the outside with glue and sawdust. When the glue dries you will have to touch up the light colored sawdust line with a little stain.

The bass pictured here was made in France in the second half of the Nineteenth Century by George Lotte, who worked under J. B. Vuillaume, as labeled.

Chapter 17

Self Service Repairs

When I wrote my first book, *"The Setup and Repair of the Double Bass for Optimum Sound"* I was against an owner doing any kind of repair to their instrument because I remembered what my then junior partner, Bill Merchant, had said, "Some of our best customers do their own work." By that he meant that they had attempted a repair for which they were not qualified and in so doing had made a subsequent repair by a professional more difficult, longer, and more costly to the owner.

Since then I have modified my position on that a bit. Over the years since my book was first published reports have been trickling in via word of mouth and letters about successful repairs. There was the story of one of Bill Merchant's clients visiting the repair shop of a general repairer and seeing an open bass on the workbench and my open book beside it. That was very gratifying. I know of a client who buys Chinese basses wholesale, sets them up for playing and then sells them at retail. And finally, I received a letter from a man who rescued a bass that had been languishing in someone's cellar for forty years. The bass was open and cracked, but he bought it for $500. He then took it to a repairer who told him it would cost several thousand dollars to restore.

Upon hearing that he took the bass back home with him. He was an amateur wood worker who was familiar with woods and wood working tools, so he decided to attempt the restoration himself. He bought my book, did the work over several months, and when finished, reported that the bass sounded great. So it can be done.

But if you want to try something like this, first you must have a good grounding in the use of wood working tools. For example, you must know that you plane in only one direction. After you have finished the stroke you must lift the plane off the work. Return it to its original position in preparation for the next stroke. You do not slide the plane back and forth across the work. When you have finished you lay the plane down on its side, never on the blade side.

So if you want to try doing your own work following the instructions in my books, first learn the proper use of your tools. Especially learn how to sharpen the cutting tools. Most lutherie techniques do not work unless the blade is really sharp. High schools used to have a course called Shop in which you were introduced to wood working tools, their proper use and proper care. Try to find such a course. Or try to get some good instruction from a carpenter or cabinet maker. Go to your local library and start researching and reading. There are two magazines about woodworking which you can read. One is called *Fine Woodworking* and the other, a British magazine, is called *Woodwork*. Do not attempt any repair until you are comfortable with the tools in your hand.

While you can repair open seams, cracks, make a bridge, and perhaps even install a new bass bar, there are certain repairs which you should not attempt under any circumstance because they are just too technical, difficult and involved. Such repairs are, for example, the grafting of a new scroll on an existing neck; inlays of missing pieces of wood; making and installing a new neck.

But if you go slowly and carefully, use the correct strength of hide glue, and follow my books you won't go too far wrong. And if you make a mistake you can always undo the repair with steam or warm water or a mixture of warm water and white vinegar.

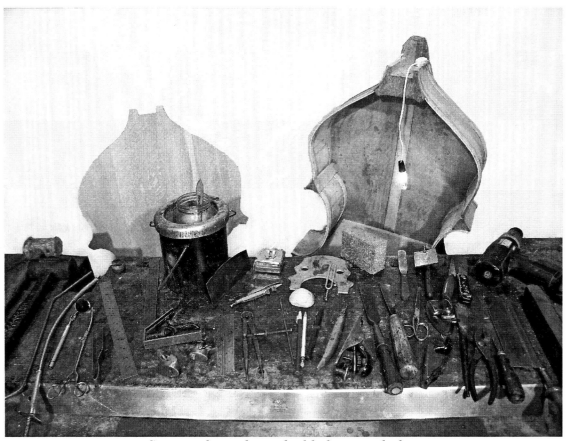

Some tools used in a double bass work shop.

However, you must do your homework, get some proficiency in the use of woodworking tools, and remember to go slowly and carefully. Don't rush into anything without first knowing exactly what you are going to do and how you are going to do it. Plan out everything first, have all the things you need for a particular repair at hand, then go to work. But before you start, be sure you have a work plan which you can follow. Don't get carried away and try something that is beyond your capabilities. If you need some advice try to find a friendly repairer willing to help. While it is almost impossible for you to destroy your bass, you can turn a subsequent repair by a professional into a major problem. So keep this in mind when you work. Remember, you can't run until you first learn to walk. And good luck.

Chapter 18

White Glue Warning

Don't use it on any part of a bass. There are three reasons for this. 1) It tends to *creep* under tension. A fingerboard glued onto a neck with white glue will eventually warp forward. 2) It is basically *irreversible* glue. Hide glue can be washed or steamed off later on, but white glue sinks into the pores of the wood and is almost impossible to remove. If hide glue is used later on it will produce only a surface instead of a molecular bond because the white glue already in the wood prevents the hide glue from sinking in and producing a molecular bond.

White glue, in comparison to hide glue, is a rather rubbery type of glue. For years repairmen have used white glue for cleats. They believed that the rubbery quality of the glue would accommodate the weather related expansion and contraction of the wood to which the cleat was glued. They thus hoped to prevent a corner of a cleat from coming loose later on and buzzing because of this movement.

When a note is being played on a bass the vibrations of that note are traveling through the wood at about 6000 miles per hour. In a brand new bass those vibrations are unhindered by cleats, producing a smooth quick flow through the wood. However, cleats act like rocks in a stream. Even if the water goes over the rocks the flow is now no longer smooth but turbulent and slower. The bigger the rock, the greater the turbulence will be. A lot of rocks, as in rapids, destroy smooth flow completely leading to slower flow and thus some loss of sound.

But with white glue something else even worse happens. The white glue, being somewhat rubbery, soaks up some of those vibrations and does not pass them on. To illustrate this point let us take two ten-foot long rods, one of metal, the other of rubber. While we tap on one end we will place a listener at the other end. With the metal rod the listener will hear even the slightest tap. With the rubber one the listener will hear nothing or next to nothing because the rubber has absorbed the tap vibrations. It would appear that the amount of vibrations soaked up by a little white glue is infinitesimal, but when you consider that less than one half of one percent of the energy put into a bass ever comes back out as sound even the slightest loss is damaging to the volume of the bass.

3) White glue robs the bass of needed sound by *absorbing* it instead of passing it on. When you consider that there may be as many as 60 or more cleats in the top alone, each glued on by that little rubber pad of white glue, each soaking up a little bit of energy, the loss in sound can be noticeable. Hide glue, being hard set glue, will not absorb energy but will pass it on.

David Brownell points out another problem. Depending on the number and size of the cleats we can get an out-of-phase problem. White glue introduces a slight delay or 'dwell time'. The return impulse from the cleat against the primary wood of the top can be slightly out of phase with the original vibration robbing it of some of its strength.

Moreover, with large patches we have a further complication with disruption of the sound path because of partial reflection at the white glue layer.

Do not use white glue.

It was at this point that a colleague who had read a draft of this chapter, an excellent repairer in his own right, wondered whether what I had just written would stand up to scientific scrutiny. Good question. So I called up my good friend and colleague, Gary Rickman of Homewood, Illinois, a suburb of Chicago, whom I knew had some pretty sophisticated electronic equipment, and explained the problem to him. Gary is a violin maker by trade but a bass repair specialist by popular demand.

He came up with his first experiment. He took two pieces of almost identical wood whose fundamental tap tones differed by only one hertz. He tapped them in front of a microphone hooked up to his analytical equipment and observed the responses of the tap tone and the higher harmonics. He then brushed hide glue on one piece of wood and the latest version aliphatic resin glue (by far the most common currently used) on the other, and when the glues were dry he tapped again. No apparent difference

He then brushed them with the glues again. This time there was a significant difference. The peak of the hide glue wood was sharper and higher and the higher harmonics were still present. The peak on the aliphatic resin glued board had sagged and rounded out and the higher harmonics had all but disappeared. The hide glue had stiffened the wood making it easier for sound waves (including the highs) to pass through while the aliphatic resin glue had either softened the wood or, more likely, acted like a muting blanket on it.

But all that this proved was that a small bit of aliphatic resin glue such as used on the well spaced cleats of only one crack *might* do no harm. However, a lot of aliphatic resin glue, such as in an overlay patch, appeared to be deleterious to the wood to which it was applied. It would *probably* change the quality of the sound response because of the loss of highs and also make it less in volume as indicated by the lowering and rounding of the peak of the fundamental. But none of this proved what would happen to sound if two pieces of wood were glued together with the two different glues.

So he tried another experiment. For all who have played croquet you know that if you place your ball right next to your opponent's ball, anchor it with your foot, then whack your ball with your mallet, the opponent's ball will go flying across the field because of the transferred energy.

He glued two pieces of wood together like a sandwich with hide glue and another two pieces with aliphatic resin glue. He then put one pair of glued woods on a smooth counter top, placed a quarter in front of the pair of wood pieces, and whacked the top piece of the glued pieces with a small hammer on a swing. The quarter would go flying across the counter top. It was hoped that the quarter would not fly as far with the aliphatic resin glued pieces of wood because that glue had absorbed energy. Unfortunately, there were too many variables over which he had no control, and the experiment was inconclusive because with the same pieces of wood sometimes the quarter would fly off the end of the board and sometimes it would only move a few inches.

Gary believes that no matter what scientific experiment he devises the old school repairers will find some way of disproving the results because they hate to admit that they have been doing something wrong for years. Even Albert Einstein spent twenty years of his life trying to disprove Heisenberg's Uncertainty Principle because he could not conceive of a universe that was not completely ordered.

But there is one fact that overrides the importance of any and all scientific tests. It is this. The use of white glues leaves an *irreversible* repair because no matter how long you try

to steam out the old glue there will always be a milky residue of glue, which can be wiped off with a paper towel, showing there is still some old white glue in the wood. Hide glue will not bond with this residual white glue, and you will be left with only a surface bond, not a molecular and stronger one. This should be sufficient deterrent not to use white glues.

Steaming off old hide glue leaves some old hide glue in the wood with which new hide glue will indeed bond.

Gary also believed that no self-respecting bass player would allow the use of chemical glue on a two hundred year old fine Italian bass, but would prefer the use of tried and true over the centuries hide glue. I believe he is right.

David Brownell did a series of experiments of sound transmission and reached the same conclusion as Gary Rickman.

Don't use white glue!

Bass made in Faenza, Italy in December, 1925 by Fausto Casalini, as labeled. Its lion's head is pictured on page 63.

Chapter 19

Mission Impossible

Until just a few weeks ago I had always believed that there was nothing so terribly wrong with a bass that it could not be repaired somehow or other. Then a friend of mine brought me a plywood bass where the plies had come unglued in many places and in very large wide strips. Furthermore, there were places where all three of the plies had come unglued.

It was then that I realized that I had been wrong. There was no way this bass could be repaired that I could think of. The problem was this - the areas that had to be glued were so extensive that it would take some time to get glue in everywhere. Then it would take quite a bit of time to clamp the entire area. In the meantime as soon as the glue hit the thin plies they would start to warp, expand, and deform.

I thought that possibly instead of using individual clamps it might be possible to do what a repairer (who had recently graduated from repairing small instruments to repairing basses) had done. He did not have the long clamps necessary to reach in from the edge of the top to places near the center seam. So, instead, he placed sandbags over the glued area and then placed a long wooden bar over the bags from one side of the top to the other. Then he clamped the bar down on either end, which put pressure on the sandbags and whatever he was gluing underneath. Quite ingenious.

(By the way, if you make a plaster of Paris mold/caul of the top you can use this method to line up a difficult crack in the top. First, slightly dampen the inside of the top along the crack, cover the crack area with a little piece of plastic, and then place warm sandbags over the crack, and press the bags down with the wooden bar. This will help line up the crack.)

But I realized that even this would take too much time. I thought about epoxy glue, but this, too, had a problem. Epoxy glue does not spread out. I would have to place it on by hand all over the entire area. Five minute epoxy would set up before I was finished placing all of it. There is a slower setting type of epoxy. But how would I use just exactly the correct amount of glue – not too thick, not too thin – especially when I could not see all the work area?

I finally decided that there was no way I could think of to repair the bass. If you have an answer I would love to hear it.

III - ANCILLARIA

CHAPTERS 20 thru 24

Chapter 20

Protocols

Selling a Bass on Consignment

When a client comes in and tells you they have a bass they want you to sell on consignment, what is the first thing you do? Offer them their choice of a cold beer or a hot coffee? No. You ask them how much they want for it.

The next thing you do is examine the instrument very carefully to determine if what they want is too high or too low. I emphasize the fact that you must be very careful in your examination because the ultimate price for the bass will be determined in part by the condition it is in. You don't want any hidden defect to show up later at just the wrong moment.

If there is anything that should be done to the bass to make it more saleable suggest that it should be done now. In this case I always collected this cost of repair after the bass had been sold. The cost of the repair should be figured into the offering price. Always recommend new strings. Otherwise it's like trying to sell a used Mercedes-Benz with old spark plugs. If the owner doesn't want to spend this money advise them that this will lower the asking price for the bass. But it's up to them.

Next try to determine country of origin and approximate date of construction. The amount of oxidation of the interior of the wood is a good clue as to age. Examine the label, if there is one, to try to find out if it is authentic or not. Finally, if it is at all possible, try to decide the name of the maker. This last is very important because a 'name' bass commands a higher selling price than an anonymous one.

Then, with your knowledge of the current market, talk over with the owner what you think you can sell the bass for. Ask them if they are in a hurry to sell or can they afford to wait. This will affect the ultimate selling price of the bass.

Finally, discuss the commission you wish to charge for your services. This should be over and above the lowest price the owner will accept so that on sale they will be guaranteed no less than what they wish to sell the instrument for and you will get your commission.

The last thing you do is give the owner your signed paper acknowledging your receipt of the bass and whatever selling price has been agreed upon and any other pertinent information such as repairs, etc. And good luck to both of you.

Chapter 21

Travel Tip

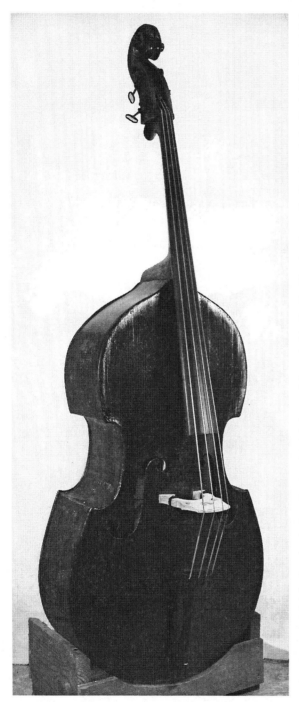

If you are like most bass players you don't like playing on the bass du jour when you arrive somewhere. So your bass travels in an old wooden coffin case or a modern hard plastic one. Don't have 100% confidence in the fact that it will arrive in one piece. I have seen several damaged basses come out of various carriers. The carrier was either dropped or received such a severe blow that the bass inside was cracked.

There is nothing you can do to prevent this type of accident from happening, but there is something you can do to minimize the damage. If a bass undergoes some type of severe shock the chances that a crack running from the bottom of the bass up through the sound post area are much greater if the bass is in full tension than if the bass were only in partial tension.

Before you place the bass in the carrier loosen the strings. If you use gut strings loosen them about three half turns. If you use metal ones loosen them about four or five half turns. If you use synthetics such as Obligatos loosen the strings ten half turns. This will keep the sound post upright under normal circumstances during travel. But if you find the sound post rolling around inside the bass when you open up the carrier, this is much better than major damage to the instrument.

Here's hoping you and your instrument will always arrive in one piece.

The bass pictured here was made by Anthony Posch in Vienna in 1729, as labeled.

Chapter 22

The Repairer's Oath

The previous two chapters have been a prelude to this one. In my first book I wrote, "I have always considered the bass to be a living sentient thing, and I the bass doctor." I have been thinking about my father, who was a very famous doctor in his day. Before he could begin to practice he had to swear to the Hippocratic Oath. If I was a doctor to basses why shouldn't there be a repairer's oath. So I have written one. Hippocrates was considered the founder of modern medicine but since there is no father of repair I have simply called this The Repairer's Oath. It is modeled after the Hippocratic Oath.

- I swear to fulfill to the best of my ability and judgment, this covenant.

- First, I will do no damage.

- I will respect the hard won scientific and empirical gains of those in whose footsteps I walk, and gladly share such knowledge as is mine with those who are to follow.

- I will apply, for the benefit of the instruments, all measures that are required, avoiding the trap of over repair.

- I will not be ashamed to say, "I know not," nor will I fail to call in my colleagues when the skills of another are needed for an instrument repair.

- I will never make a repair that is irreversible, and I will not use 'white glue' just because it is easy and convenient to use, but will always use the glue tried and found true over the centuries – hide glue.

- May I always act so as to preserve the finest traditions of my calling and may I long experience the joy of healing those instruments which need my help. Let me so endeavor to lead my life and do my work that when I come to die even the undertaker will be sorry.

Chapter 23

The Must Be 3 C's

I have written this chapter because by the time this reaches the public I will be 83, and, therefore, this will most likely be the last thing that I write.

I have been thinking about what makes a really good bass player. I don't mean the top ten in the world, for they are unfathomable geniuses. I mean the principal symphony bassists and the always in demand jazz players. Talent, of course. Dedication and burning desire, of course. But I have decided it's the little things that make the difference. I have called these the Must Be 3 C's.

These players must be Careful. They must be careful with their intonation. They must be careful with their timing, and they must be careful with their volume. All three demand great care.

They must be Critical. They must be constantly critical of their performance, for without this they cannot and will not become better and better.

And finally, they must be Curious. They must be curious about different chord progressions and substitutions; curious about different and new fingerings; curious about different bowings; curious about better sound; curious about anything that will make them a better player. When they do something that makes it easier to play or gives them a better sound, they must be curious as to why. As I have said before, "why" is the most important word in the English language because without it there is no progress.

Well, it's the same with repairers. They must be very careful with their work. It must be clean and it must be practical for the best sound. They must constantly criticize their work so as to try to improve it wherever possible. And, most importantly, when they do something that improves the sound of a bass, they must be curious as to why it improved the sound. The converse is also true. Like doctors, they must be constantly aware of new techniques that do things better.

These are the little things that make the difference between a good cabinet-maker type repairer and a truly gifted one.

In repairing for Optimum Sound less is more. It's also the little things that make the big difference.

OK, you now know what it takes to make a superior repairer, but how do you find one? First, ask everyone you know who plays the bass who their repairer is. Second, ask them how their bass sounded after the last repair. Did it sound worse? Did it sound the same or with little improvement, or did it sound noticeably better? If it sounded worse, scratch that name off your list immediately. If it sounded the same or only slightly better, save that name to use in emergencies. If it sounded noticeably better, that's the one for you.

Chapter 24

The Quest

Just because I don't wear shining armor and ride around on a white horse doing battle with old school repairers trying to get them to change their thinking and their ways doesn't mean I don't have a quest. I do. And the bass is my fair lady for whom I am ready to do anything I can to serve and protect her.

In my 375 page book, *"The Setup and Repair of the Double Bass for Optimum Sound,"* I had three ideas that I wanted everyone to know about.

The first was this: The bass is not an overgrown violin or a big brother to the cello. It is a separate and unique instrument, and it must be treated that way. The bass cannot be repaired like a violin or a cello. It must have its own unique methods of repair. Repairs that will work on the smaller instruments absolutely will not work on a bass. In my book I discussed the whys and wherefores of this statement and told how certain repairs should be done. The less wood you put in repairs the better. Less is more.

For decades I have been preaching the sermon that you can't repair a bass the same way you can any of the smaller instruments of the string section, and I have been pooh-poohed by some big name small instrument repairers for saying it. This is what I said in my first book- "It is important to note than in violin repair manuals there are certain types of repairs that will work quite well on smaller instruments. These, however, either will not work at all on basses, or they will impede the ability of the bass to function at its optimum level." Recently Bill Merchant lent me a copy of a book published in 1988 by Hans Weisshaar and Margaret Shipman entitled *Violin Restoration – A Manual for Violin Makers*. This book is an excellent landmark exploration and explanation of violin repair. But in it I found more than a few repairs that will work on a violin that absolutely will not work on a bass. They range from either being dangerous to the bass or to being an impediment to its ability to produce a proper sound.

One in particular struck me immediately. I quote from pages 4 and 5: "4) The table (top or front - my insertion) is separated from the ribs by inserting an opening knife in a seam (joint). The weakest joints are usually on the upper right edge and chinrest positions, (translating this into bass-speak means at the neck and end blocks.), due to perspiration and body contact. Begin opening at the upper or lower bouts unless some other seam is already open."

The explanation for removing a top continues on for two more paragraphs before this next sentence: "Next, free a center bout."

If you do this to a bass in summer you may get away with it, but if you do it in winter you are courting disaster. I am now going to relate an experience, which I wrote about in my first book. My mentor, Josef Cillecek, always told me what to do but never why. He told me always to start to take a top off by opening the center bout first. In the beginning of my career as a repairman I did so with about the first six or so repairs that I had to do. One day a bass came into my shop in which the top was open from the endpin block by about six inches. "Aha, I thought. Now I've caught me a break. I'll just continue on up the seam with my knife." I hadn't gone more than about two inches when there was a loud pop and a crack in the top from the bottom of the bass up to the F hole suddenly appeared. Then I knew why you always start at the center bout. The back had shrunk so much that it was pulling the ribs in where they were attached to the back. This meant that the ribs attached to the top were pulling out against the top with considerable force – enough to initiate a split in the top. That was the last time I ever did that.

But this is a prime example of something that will work well on a violin that is destructive to a bass. Don't do it.

The second was this: I was trying to get people to think in a different way about the bass and its problems. If people are willing to change their thinking about the bass, the instrument will benefit immeasurably. The new knowledge as to how a bass actually functions has to be accepted and understood for the betterment of the instrument.

The third was this: I was putting forth what I now call **Traeger's Principle**. It is this:

When a bass is being played every part of the instrument, from the top of the scroll to the tip of the endpin is vibrating. (Understanding this will make you a better repairer.)

Corollary number one: For Optimum Sound to occur every part must be vibrating at an optimum level and in sync (in phase) with its neighbors.

Corollary number two: Maximum is **not** necessarily optimum. For example, when a neck is too thin it will vibrate at maximum, not optimum level, siphoning off energy from the strings that should have gone into the body of the bass. Furthermore, this level of energy is usually at a lower frequency that does not reinforce the fixed resonance frequencies of the instrument and thus will further divert energy from the strings that should have gone into the body of the bass. The result is a loss of sound. A similar loss in sound can occur when the neck is not securely glued into the body.

My quest is to get this information out to as many people as possible – repairers and players. Only then will the bass really sing. Only then will players really get the most out of their instruments.

Word has begun to trickle in from players and repairers that my ideas actually do work. I can't tell you how gratifying this is. It lets me know that I haven't done battle for nothing. I am beginning to win and so is my beloved fair lady, the bass.

58

Epilogue

I was delighted to hear what a controversy my statement about gamba versus violin corners has stirred up, although I hope it does not detract from the rest of my book. From controversy comes knowledge. On page 2 of my first book I wrote, "Basses with violin rather than gamba corners *generally* have a darker sound." I did not say by how much, and generally does not mean always. It means more often than not even if that is only 51 percent of the time. This is my theory and not something to be written in stone.

When a bass is properly tuned up it is in tension but it is a static state - no movement. As soon as you pull a string to one side either with a finger or with bow hair the bass starts to move. This is a dynamic state. Let us consider what happens to the body of the bass just before that pulled string is let go.

The pulled string exerts two simultaneous forces on the bass. One is a tensile force on the top of the neck block and the top of the endpin block, pulling them together. The other is a compressive force exerted on the top of the bass by the bridge. This latter force distorts the top by pushing the bass bar and top down. Most of this downward distortion occurs near the E string F hole. However, there is some residual distortion in the top, which occurs beyond the ends of the bass bar where the curve of the top changes from convex to concave. This distortion is also downward. The downward distortion of the top at these points aids in pulling the neck block and endpin block together.

This force can be measured in pounds and its direction depicted by arrows called force vectors. So on the top plate draw an imaginary line down from the neck block pointing to the middle of the top plate. Draw another arrow from the endpin block up to the middle of the top plate. This means that the top is in compression because the tops of the blocks have been pulled closer together by the dynamic force imposed on the string.

Let us consider the ribs when the tops of the blocks are being pulled closer together. This exerts a compressive force on the tops of the ribs. Draw imaginary arrows along the tops of the ribs from the end blocks to the centers of the C bouts. The only way the upper and lower bout ribs can relieve this compressive force is to bend outwards because that is the way they are curved. But what happens to the C bout ribs? They are being pushed together by those arrows you drew. The only way they can relieve this pressure is to bend inwards because that is the way they are curved.

Let us now examine what happens to the top while all this bending is going on. At the upper bouts the ribs have bent outwards. This exerts a tensile force on the top pulling the top flatter between the upper bout ribs and adding to the downward movement of the concave ends of the top. The same thing is happening to the top plate between the lower bout ribs.

But what is happening to the top plate in between the C bout corners? The C bouts are bending in. The only way the top can relieve this pressure is to bend up. This movement here is further helped along by the fact that the top is in compression trying to push the top plate up. It is the upward pressure that helps the bass bar push the top back up when the string is released.

Here is the difference between the motions of the gamba and violin corner ribs. With gamba corners the ribs curve and bend in only one direction - outward. With violin corners the ribs bend outward where they curve outward and they bend inward where they curve inward. This means the inward bending of the C bouts starts where the curve of the upper and lower bout ribs change direction from an outward curve to an inward one.

If you have trouble visualizing this take a piece of typewriter paper and bend it a bit until you have imposed a curve in it. This is a representation of the rib of an upper or lower bout ending in a gamba corner. Now put one side of the curved paper on top of a table with the outward curve facing you, and stabilize the place where it touches the table so that it won't slip around. Push the top ends a bit and watch what happens to the outward curve in the paper. It bends further out. This is exactly what happens to an upper or lower bout rib. Now reverse the paper so that the curve is now facing away from you. What you are now looking at is not the entire rib but *only that part of the violin corner of the rib* where the curve is inward. Push the top of the paper again. The paper/rib now bends inward, and the curve begins exactly where you start to push.

This is the important part. It means the distance between where the ribs of a violin corner bass start to bend the C bout inward is 3-4 inches wider apart than where the ribs of a gamba corner bass start to bend the C bout inward. This means that that part of the top plate that is being pushed upward is wider (or longer, if you will) in a violin corner bass than a gamba corner bass! The *wider* that part of the top plate is, the easier it is for longer wave vibrations to *exist*. The longer the wave the lower is the frequency. The longer the xylophone block the lower the note. That is why tympani will sound lower and darker than a snare drum no matter how much you tighten the head. No matter how you detune the head a snare will never sound like a tympani. That is why the low notes on a grand piano sound richer and fuller than the same notes on an upright. You will not hear this lower frequency sound as a dominant sound. Instead it will be added onto the existing sound spectrum and will be heard as a coloring part of it. This is one of the reasons that Gagliano basses are so prized for their tone because he made the C bouts longer than usual thus affecting a longer area of the top between them.

But what is happening to the back while all this is going on? In the forty years I have been repairing I have seen thousands of basses, and in every one the back was of a stiffer wood than the top no matter what wood it was, be it maple, pear wood, or poplar. Also the back is almost twice as thick as the top. Because of this the excursions of the vibrations are much less, and so the back acts more or less like a platform on which the ribs and top move. The endpin and neck blocks do not rotate about their centers so that the bottom of the blocks pulls outward while the top pushes in. Rather, the place where the blocks are glued to the back acts like a fulcrum fixed to the back allowing the top of the blocks to move back and forth distorting the ribs and the top as they move.

This is not the only motion the top goes through when the bass is being played but it is an important one. Does shape affect sound? Yes, but so do a lot of other things. That is why I said 'generally' not 'always'.

All things being equal (and they never are because of differences in plate thickness, placement and design of bridge and sound post, design and number - outside as well as inside - of linings) violin corner basses will *generally* be darker than gamba corner basses, if only slightly, and 'generally' means only 51% or more.

This analysis may be flawed because my degree is in Civil Engineering not in Audio Engineering. But it is an educated guess. Anyhow, it works for me. If anyone can come up with a different and better theory I would be privileged to read it especially if it differs from mine.

However, there are other factors which aid in the development of darker sound in violin corner basses. Here is what my good friend and colleague, David Brownell, has to say.

"The rib structure (for the same rib thickness) of the violin-style rib garland shows a little less rib stiffness toward the corners because of the transition between outward and inward curve, compared with the single-curvature gamba-style rib. Further, there almost always is a difference between actual corner stiffness due to the shape of the glued-in corner block. (Disregarding those Saxon and Bohemian instruments that have no corner block at all; those reinforced, if at all, by a fold of parchment or linen glued into the corner.) With corner blocks, however, the gamba-style corner usually has a triangular fillet of relatively small dimension and equal gluing surface areas against each rib section. The violin-pattern corner block, however, if not built with merely the Saxon-style partition block may not be too much deeper for the surface glued to the C bout rib, but typically extends half again to as much as twice that of the block width along the surface of the upper or lower rib section. The proportions of this block affect the tone color of the instrument as well as the power of the lower register. The stiffer construction of a rib corner constructed with Italian or Mittenwald pattern corner blocks seems to better let the plate 'pump' to produce good low tones, while also giving a good top register to the bass. The proportion of block with the narrow edge extending about 1/3 of the way around the tight curl at the ends of the C bout seems to filter better the 'dark' sound than is the case with a 'narrower' corner block proportion."

But why do I include all this here? It is to show that, along with all the other parts, the top and ribs are moving, so the less that is done to impede this movement, the better the bass will sound. It is also to show that a very few strap cleats may successfully be used on the back where the motion is less.

Finally, I wrote this to reiterate **Traeger's Principle**, which is the fundamental foundation for everything I have written about the bass.

Traeger's Principle states: WHEN A BASS IS BEING PLAYED, EVERYTHING IS VIBRATING, FROM THE TIP OF THE SCROLL TO THE TIP OF THE ENDPIN.

First corollary: For Optimum Sound to occur every part of the bass must be vibrating at an optimum level and in sync (in phase) with its neighbors so that it reinforces the vibrations of its neighbors rather than conflicting with them.

Second corollary: Maximum is **not** necessarily Optimum. (For an explanation of this see the Prologue.)

This is the mantra for the bass's Optimum Sound. Understand this and all else follows naturally.

The bass pictured here was made in England by John Betts in 1833, as labeled. The combination of violin corners, flat arching and broad wide bouts make most English basses sound quite dark.